I0843099

Roads

All Roads Lead to Roam

by
The Lonesome Hillbilly

Books by the same author

The Book on Motorcycle Camping
How to Live on the Road Full Time

Places: I'm Going to Go Back There, Some Day

Roads: All Roads Lead to Roam

Friends: Two-Legs, Four-Legs, Six-Legs, Wings and Roots

Visions: Things and Ideas Found in the Wild

Elements: Elemental, Elementary

Things in Heaven and Earth
Essays from Places, Roads, Friends, Visions and Elements
with full-color illustrations

Dedicated to
Donna, and Rico,
and all of the other flagmen
and their road crews
who keep the roads there for me to use

Contents

Gipsy Vans
by Rudyard Kipling

Unless you come of the gipsy stock
  That steals by night and day,
Lock your heart with a double lock
  And throw the key away.
Bury it under the blackest stone
  Beneath your father's hearth,
And keep your eyes on your lawful own
  And your feet to the proper path.
    Then you can stand at your door and mock
      When the gipsy vans come through...
    For it isn't right that the Gorgio stock
      Should live as the Romany do.

Unless you come of the gipsy blood
  That takes and never spares,
Bide content with your given good
  And follow your own affairs.
Plough and harrow and roll your land,
  And sow what ought to be sowed;
But never let loose your heart from your hand,
  Nor flitter it down the road!
    Then you can thrive on your boughten food
      As the gipsy vans come through...
    For it isn't nature the Gorgio blood
      Should love as the Romany do.

Unless you carry the gipsy eyes
  That see but seldom weep,
Keep your head from the naked skies
  Or the stars'll trouble your sleep.
Watch your moon through your window-pane
  And take what weather she brews;
But don't run out in the midnight rain
  Nor home in the morning dews.
    Then you can buddle and shut your eyes
      As the gipsy vans come through...
    For it isn't fitting the Gorgio ryes
      Should walk as the Romany do.

Unless you come of the gipsy race
  That counts all time the same,
Be you careful of Time and Place
  And Judgment and Good Name:
Lose your life for to live your life
  The way that you ought to do;
And when you are finished, your God and your wife
  And the Gipsies'll laugh at you!
    Then you can rot in your burying place
      As the gipsy vans come through...
    For it isn't reason the Gorgio race
      Should die as the Romany do.

Introduction: Roads

The Road is my home, in a very literal sense. It is also the most important thing in my life. While I spend most of my time not actually on a road, the places I stay are only rooms in the great mansion called the Rocky Mountains, and the roads are hallways between rooms. Many, many doors open off of the hallways, some closed, some open. I look through the open ones as I pass, sometimes stepping inside for a moment. I also pause to admire the great art, paintings and sculptures and vases and knick-knacks, adornments crowding the long, wide hallways. Many other hallways branch off in all directions, each with its own plethora of doorways and art. Sometimes I follow them, sometimes not. The Winchester Mystery House is tame and mundane compared to *my* mansion!

There are three uses, in my view, for the Road. The primary use, the obvious one, the one for which it was created, is to make it easier, faster and safer, to get from Here to There. Whether moving one's self, a cargo, or just information, whether moving only half a mile or all of the way across a continent, the Road is the original tool for the movement.

The second use can be viewed as a subset of the first: To see and visit and experience places on the way from Here to There. What makes it secondary is that few people would travel a hundred miles just to view some historical marker or site or a historical person's birthplace. Some people will, and their number is growing rapidly as our wealth in time, opportunity and money increases. I have done it myself, detouring a day out of my way specifically and only to visit a small and specialized museum. I have done so several times.

The third use is simply to travel, to be On the Road. Often, this is a subset of the second use. The old marketing slogan "Getting there is half the fun" is an example. It refers to the things one can see and do while en route to whatever the destination may be. But there is also a small group who treasure the mere fact of travelling. Most are bikers, for whom being on a bike is its own justification. My favorite example: I sometimes have to ride on my bike thirty miles just to do the laundry. On the other hand, I get to ride on my bike thirty miles, just to do the laundry! Sure, we see the sights along the way, and often stop to see them better, but riding the most monotonous highway, such as the country routes in the movie *Brazil,* or even riding in a fog, is better than not riding at all. I have done that, too. Try I-10 between Quartzsite and Phoenix, or I-80 through Nevada.

My book *Places* is about the first use: the best Theres that I have gotten to. This book is mostly about the second, sights and scenes along the way, with just a touch of the third (it is difficult to describe comprehensibly the allure of just riding for the sake of riding). Some roads are packed with wayside attractions; here you will read about a thirty-six mile road that you should take all day to traverse, because there is so much to see on the way. I know others roads, long ones, that are only good for the third use, except for one or two scenes en route, and those scenes are the only mention included.

I have been to all of the places described; the photographs are all my own. The impressions recorded are what I received. Actually, only a small part of what I received; I could fill an entire book with a photographically detailed description and account of my thoughts about a single scene, but it would be fearfully boring. Your own impressions will be different, *should* be different. Just go there and see, for yourself.

What They Are

The Road

Tracks, paths, trails, traces, roads, highways, freeways, even rivers and streams. They are all the same thing, differing only in size and in quality. A track you may not even notice; only a few travelers, often only one, has used it. With enough traffic, it will become a path, the way worn, plants trampled to nothing, few if any branches or rocks intruding. In time, it may become permanent, a trail or a trace. And if it is frequently used, it will qualify as a road. Humans will upgrade theirs, and grade them and pave them with gravel or tar or concrete, and the bigger and more heavily used become highways and freeways. Several of these cement ribbons stretch all the way across a continent. They usually lie where someone walked, following the course he happened to use, usually avoiding obstructions and trending more or less towards the objective. Sometimes they are planned in advance. The Romans made good roads. They made them straight. When a hill stood in the way, they went over it or through it, almost never around it. They made them to endure. They dug wide ditches, then filled them with big rocks, then small rocks, gravel and sand, and laid flat stones on top. They embedded the paving stones in cement of some sort, even lead. Yes, they poured molten lead and set the stones in it. Or perhaps they set the stones, then poured lead to fill in the spaces. They lined the roads with drainage ditches and culverts and built bridges where needed. They were the best roads in the world, and were not surpassed for well over a millenium, not until some old Scotsman named MacAdam revived their technique, replacing the top stones with a layer of asphalt and gravel. Most modern engineering works would not much impress the ancient Roman engineers, but the interstate highways and multiple overlapping intersections... The Romans would regard them with deep appreciation. And old MacAdams' roads continued to improve. The original interstate highways from the 1950's were good, were superb for their time. Why, you could cross the country at fifty miles per hour! Now, they would be second-rate at best. Today I cruised for most of the day at eighty miles per hour, and only three times did I need to slow when the road became rough and uneven for short stretches. And I thought nothing of it, for it was normal, and to be expected. But suddenly I noticed it. I paid attention. I had a vision.

With all the differences in size and composition, they are all, paths, roads, freeways, all still the same thing: they are lines of communication. They are routes from Here to There. They are the arteries and veins of the animal world on which almost everything that moves travels. Birds and insects and fish will go where they will. The ground-bound will also pass where they will, but only for a short distance, for a whim, a moment's convenience. For regular destinations, for passage from den to water-hole, or home to work, or city to vacation, for these there is The Road.

There are not many roads. In the Americas, there are a few hundred islands, each of which has a road. But the mainland, North and South, has only one. It is a network, millions of miles of road, stretching from the Arctic Sea to the Antarctic, and from Atlantic to Pacific, winding, branching, joining, the web of a psychotic spider, made of dirt and mud and gravel and tar and concrete, even of iron, known by tens of thousands of names and numbers, and bearing millions upon millions of travelers. It is never idle, always in use by millions of people at any instant of any day. It is constantly degrading and falling apart and being built and rebuilt and demolished and repaired. There are many men who spend their entire lives building The Road, and it will never be done, even if all travel should take to the air, for we will still need it to walk upon. Yes, we will. For all of our tens of thousands of years of technological advance, we still walk the same way the first Cro-Magnan did, and it takes us just as long to cross a hundred yards as it took him. Asia, Europe and Africa have one. Only one, shared among the three. Australia has one. And Ireland. And Jamaica, and Dominica, and Madagascar, and every other inhabited island. One road each. And all the same, in essence. All incarnations of the idea of The Road.

People wonder at the Great Wall of China (which is actually a road). They are awe-struck by the Pyramids at Giza. Not me. Those are minor works, rather small, quickly and easily built. I save my fascination for the greatest, the largest work in all of the history of Mankind. I reserve it for The Road. For it is bigger than everything else put together. It has consumed more man-hours and more resources over the past few thousand years than all of the rest taken together. And it has delivered more value, more service as well. The history of mankind could be expressed as the history of The Road, and that would probably be the most accurate expression. There were times when one village would have bumper crops, and another village twenty miles away, whose crops had failed, would starve, simply because there was no road, no way to move the surplus food to where it was needed. Ancient Rome expanded its influence till it became a great empire, which it could not have done without The Road. The American Indians fought the white man to a standstill, then lost everything when The Road was built to and through their lands. Air travel has changed the world. Sea transport is vital for world commerce; it was to the British Empire what land roads were to the Roman. They were and are very important. But even those pale before the importance and impact of The Road.

And here I am, riding The Road, casually travelling over three hundred miles just to be in a new place, and thinking it nothing special. And being so very, very wrong. True, it is nothing unique, nothing uncommon, nothing out of the ordinary. But it is special, very special. Travellers of a century and a half ago would have spent a month or more struggling over the distance I cover in half a day. Teamsters laboriously hauled wagonloads of goods over the same routes that are routine for the eighteen-wheelers I am dodging around, trucks that each carry ten times the cargo of a single wagon, and carry it a hundred times as fast. Why the difference? Because we have better, bigger, faster machines? No, because we have The Road. A modern semi-trailer could not travel at all on the old wagon roads. It would run out of fuel, even in the unlikely event it did not bog down or break. No, first comes The Road, then vehicles to make better use of it. The first road was trod out by feet, then enlarged by sledges and wagons, and improved for those sledges and wagons, until it became what it is today. But the road came first.

I look at the road almost every day. I look at it for miles, dozens of miles, hundreds of miles at a time. And I have done so for decades. I have read Bilbo's songs, *the road goes ever on and on*, and other poems and essays and odes, and even written about it myself. But until today, I never *looked* at it, I never *saw* it, never knew it for what it is: The Road. *The* Road. The incomparable majesty, and grandeur, and beauty. Now I have seen it.

And I can never forget.

Happy Trails

There are many attractions in the Wilds, especially in our National Forests and Parks. They all contain spectacular views, primeval forests, intimidating canyons, inviting valleys, endless grasslands, lakes and ponds and rivers and streams of all descriptions. Many hold unique experiences: awesome rock formations, sculpted towers and bridges and arches, splendid waterfalls, magnificent caves. They are dotted with educational opportunities: "Points of Interest", museums, explanatory signs, historical markers. More and more are offering citified distractions . . . I mean attractions . . . such as bookstores and gift shops and Imax theaters. But what is probably the best feature is the plethora of trails.

There are the long and famous trails such as the John Muir Trail and the Appalachian Trail, each of which is hundreds of miles long, and good for a day hike or an entire summer's adventure. Some are unofficial, game trails made by the local animals for their own day-to-day use. Some, especially in wilderness areas, are marked but almost unmaintained. Wilderness areas are intended to be as untouched by Man as possible; you take it as it is. Most trails lie in between, trails laid out, improved and maintained by state and federal park and forest workers. Their variety is infinite. Some have bridges, concrete or lumber or just a couple of logs, across streams and gullies; some make do with simple fords. Some handle steep slopes with a series of switchbacks, some have stairs, either concrete, or fairly regularly placed squarish stones. Brush and protruding branches are kept cut back, gullies and washouts are filled. Most are levelled to some degree. I have even seen some which are maintained by the simple expedient or driving an industrial lawnmower through every few weeks. Whatever you are looking for, whatever your limitations may be, there are trails for you, even paved ones navigable by wheelchairs.

In my youth, I traveled with a backpack. My first long journey was by inflatable canoe from the Appalachians to Oil City, Pennsylvania, where the river became too foul, then on foot the rest of the way to the Pacific. Some places I walked along the roads, but mostly, I followed the trails laid out through National Forests. I truly wish everyone could do the same, at least spend a summer hiking through wild lands. It can change your life, and surely for the better. But at the very least, spend a week or two, or at least a couple of weekends, somewhere in the woods, grasslands or deserts. You have no interest? You have no such desires? You have better, more profitable things to do? No, you do not. You *need* the experience. You cannot evaluate or appreciate or even dislike, not rationally, a thing you have never seen, never done, never experienced. Most of the eco-simps I knew in the city wanted to protect and preserve Nature, but had no idea what they were talking about. Most of their "protective" ideas were actually harmful, like the international ban on ivory sales, which only gave the elephant poachers a monopoly and raised their profit margin, because they do not have enough knowledge to make a sane decision. For example, they wanted to ban or reduce hunting, not understanding that, since we killed off most of the wolves to protect livestock, we *have* to take over their role as predators to prevent their prey from overpopulating, ruining their environment by over-grazing, and starving themselves. The most ardent conservationists I know are active hunters, men and women who get their deer every year, or fishermen who are out at the water every chance they can get. These are people who know the Wilds, who understand and cherish them.

It is easy to develop a similar understanding yourself. Take a vacation for a week or two, or over several weekends. For a few hundred dollars you can buy the basic essential gear: A tent and sleeping bag, stout hiking boots, and little else, for just a weekend. Or you can rent an RV, a small motor home or van fitted out as a camper. Or you can get a room at an outdoor lodge, a hotel intended for people who want to experience the Wilds without camping out. You do not even have to have the boots; if you limit yourself to the easier trails, sneakers will do. Just get out here and find out for yourself what it is all about.

There are trails everywhere. They are usually graded, Easy, Intermediate, Difficult, and Expert or Advanced. The Easy ones are generally little more difficult than walking down a sidewalk. They are smooth, with few or no rocks or gullies, no steep slopes, or with steps or stairs where necessary, and can be just as beautiful and interesting as any other trails. You can walk them in sandals, and many of them will accommodate a wheelchair. Intermediates can usually be walked in sneakers; Difficult and Expert require boots. Do not try a Difficult trail till you have done a few Intermediates and understand what you will be getting into. And definitely stay away from Expert trails; you will know when you are ready for them, if ever. (I expect a few macho fools will take that as a challenge and set out to prove their manliness; it may help to clean the gene pool.) A walking stick or staff is very helpful, and often necessary on the more advanced trails. Hiking boots are never a bad idea, and only a fool will neglect to bring water, and plenty of it. A camera is not vital, but if you do not bring one, you will regret it.

Some trails have a specific purpose, a destination. There is one in the Shoshone National Forest which leads, after a few miles, to a fascinating complex of waterfalls on the Middle Popo Agie River. It is rated Very Difficult (I would say only Difficult), long and with some moderately rough and steep stretches; you would be well-advised to take a staff or walking stick. The scenery along the way is very varied, from lush forest to desolate stony and scraggly grassed hills to intricate river canyon. There are a dozen or so waterfalls of all types, rock walls and river boulders carved into fantasy shapes (there is a sunstruck troll in the middle of the river). There are several benches where you can eat lunch while admiring the falls, and a series of simple bridges that take you right around the falls. Do not neglect to see that part! You do need to be in reasonably good shape (though that is true of all Intermediate trails and above), but it is well worth the hike. Do not forget to bring your camera.

I would also like to point out that this trail has a logbook at the beginning. On any trail that has one, it is a very good idea to sign in when you start, and sign out when you return. Then if you should meet with an accident (or a bear), the Rangers will know you are still up there, and send someone to find you. Also, unless you are properly equipped and truly know what you are doing, it is not a trail to take alone; no Difficult or Expert trail is.

Another of my favorite trails is the Overlook Trail at Villanueva State Park in New Mexico. It is a loop a couple of miles long that runs along the Pecos River, then up a near-vertical cliff (with several stairways of cleverly-placed local rocks), along the rim of the cliff (and at some points, right *at* the rim), then back down the other side and along the river to your starting point. There is also a short branch trail that leads to The Overlook. It is a wonderful spot for lunch under a couple of shady ramadas, with a full panorama of the surrounding mountains and high plateau. It is an Intermediate, and requires at least good sneakers, preferably boots. I strongly advise a stout staff, plenty of water, and, absolutely, a camera. The lower stretches are thickly wooded riverine, the top is arid scrub desert. There are many beautiful views along and across the valley, some fascinating wildlife areas, including a small city of wasp nests, and of course, at the top, The Overlook. There is even a Historic Site, an old stone corral (or the ruins of it) built by rebels during a revolution in the 1800s. The trail can be hiked in either direction. I recommend doing it twice, once to the left, once to the right. Why? Because the view is so different. This is another important safety point: Whenever you are hiking, wherever you may be, do *not* look only ahead. There is much of beauty on either side, of course, but the view behind you is usually very different from the view ahead. No, you did not already see it as you approached; you only saw half of it, if that. Turn around. Look back the way you came. Landmarks you noted are no longer visible, or look so different that they are not recognizable. You can easily (it has often happened, *very* often happened) be returning along the same trail, and be firmly convinced that you took a wrong turn somewhere and are lost, because nothing looks familiar. On your way up, do note landmarks ahead of you, but also turn and look behind frequently to note other landmarks, and especially look to the sides. The side ones are most important, because they will be more visible when trying to orient yourself. At least, that has been my experience. Also, from esthetics, often there will be a beautiful view looking back that was completely invisible when you passed it on the way out. Look back often, or you will miss some fine photographs.

There is such a plenitude of exquisite trails, I could fill an entire book just describing them. Maybe I will, someday. For now, I will just say there are trails of every imaginable type, suited to every taste and every need. There are trails for hiking, trails for mountain bikes, trails for off-road vehicles. There are trails that lead to special places, trails that circle back to their starting points, trails that go nowhere in particular, just wander pleasurably through the woods. Some people like to hike from one campsite to another, spending a week to go from Here to There, then back home. Some people like to take a morning or afternoon stroll, or hike somewhere for lunch, then back by a different route for dinner. I like to pack a chair, notebook, camera and lunch, and randomly walk till I reach a place that feels right. There I stop and sit, and just be there, doing nothing, merging with the Wild. Usually inspiration will come, and I will write. Often nothing happens at all, and that is just as good. The animals will come out to forage, the birds will flit and sing, and even the stupid squirrels will eventually forget about me and shut up.

Do you get it? You can do anything you want. Anything or nothing. Whatever suits your taste. But whatever it is, it is *real*. It is *actual*. It *is*. This is the original reality show, now in its five hundred millionth season. Whatever suits you, there is a trail leading to it. You just have to find it. And while you are looking, you will find many, many other things, things you had no idea existed, but will treasure for the rest of your life. If you look for them.

But you have to look.

Interstates

It would be difficult to overstate the Interstate Highway System. It is beyond doubt the greatest accomplishment of the Human Race to date. All of the ancient Seven Wonders of the World do not even begin to approach, much less equal it, even if you throw in the Great Wall of China. Only the Roman system of roads is at all comparable, and even that has been surpassed. Oh, the ancient Romans would probably disagree, and not for chauvanistic reasons. Our Interstates are smoother, and wider, and longer, but they do not last as long, and require much more maintenance, and they *wind* and *twist*, they are laid out around hills instead of over them or through them. I cannot honestly disagree with the Romans, but I will point out that our Interstates are better suited to our needs. And while they have the same primary purpose as the Roman roads, to allow swift movement of troops and war materiel, we have yet to actually use them for that purpose, and for their secondary purpose, civilian transportation, we use ours far more than the Romans used theirs.

Mainly, we use the Interstates to Get There Fast. I suppose I should say, *you* use them, for I rarely want speed. For me, being on the way is much more fun than arriving, and usually just as much fun as what I do once I am There. I like to see where I am and where I am going, and the myriad myriad sights along the way. Interstates are not especially good for this. Yes, many of them offer grand vistas and unique landmarks, but only in passing. They are not laid out with a mind to sightseeing, and only rarely can you pull over and stop without a durn good reason. Many times you must go ten or twenty or more miles before you can get off of the Interstate and stop. And even though they are intended to get you there, they rarely actually go *to* anywhere. They get you close, but then you must get off and use the lesser roads to reach your true destination. On the other hand, you are far more likely to find a motel near an Interstate exit than elsewhere. In fact, near larger settlements, you usually find a plethora, from forty-dollar cheap rooms to two-hundred-dollar-plus luxury rooms, with pool and spa and room service.

Still, some of them are beautiful. I-25 from Las Cruces to a few mile short of Albuquerque passes through some very scenic countryside. On the other hand, there is I-80 in Nevada. The natives tell me they are quite pleased with it, because it passes through the dullest, most boring land in the state, and thus discourages the duller and more boring tourists from infesting the back country. I do not completely agree. Perhaps it is just me and my viewpoints, but I do not find that area dull or boring at all; it has its own unique beauty. It is big, and only changes in details, so I suppose most city-folk, especially from Hollywood, would consider it a good insomnia cure.

If you need to get somewhere quickly, such as across Kansas and Eastern Colorado to reach the mountains, Interstates are likely your best choice. But if you wish to view the scenery, to get to know and understand the land you are passing through, get on the back roads and take your time. Even I, who live out here on the Road, begrudge hours wasted staring at three lanes of asphalt.

Highways

Interstate highways are officially differentiated from other highways; they are clearly designated as Interstates. Not because they pass between states. Not all of them do; there are Interstates in Hawaii, which cannot possibly leave the state. There are several in Los Angeles which do not even leave the city. But there are none in Alaska. Not even one. Odd. There are many highways, national highways, that pass from state to state, and are not named Interstates, such as Route 66 and Route 95. But it is more than just a name, for the official Interstates are usually better maintained. Usually. The other roads are just Highways, or less.

The biggest practical difference between the Interstates and other highways is access. You can only get on or off an Interstate (legally, that is) at specific Exits. Usually, stopping anywhere else is frowned upon. The other highways can be accessed just about anywhere. You build a farm near the highway, and you can run an access road or your driveway right up to the road. You can also pull off the highway any place the shoulder is wide enough, for whatever reason you want. Just to admire the scenery, or take a picture of that horse. Whatever. You can also drive more slowly; I have yet to see a minimum speed posted for anything but an Interstate. The landscapes around highways are usually more scenic than around Interstates, so it is good that you can drive slowly and stop when you wish.

The main difference between national and state highways is maintenance. When the maintenance crew on a US route comes to a state border, they generally just keep going. The state crew stops. This means you can identify the border with high precision. It is not where that Welcome sign is posted; it is where the pavement changes abruptly from asphalt to concrete, or where the surface changes from smooth to cracked and potholed. You can even find half potholes, where it has been filled in one state, and left untouched in the neighbor. Okay, okay, I have never actually *seen* one, but I would not be surprised.   Amused, yes, but not surprised.   Knowing bureaucracies, the conscientious worker would likely be censured and have to pay for the "wasted" filling.

The highways also pass through towns and villages, while Interstates pass above them, or at a distance. I-10 passes right through Quartzsite, Arizona, but there is at least a hundred feet of space between the pavement and the town. Many of these villages are very picturesque, some with buildings hundreds of years old, and still in use. Others have ruins, old adobes or log cabins, or planked frontier stores and saloons. Many, especially in the Southwest, boast Historical Markers explaining significant events in their history, or the closest thing that the locals can think of to a significant event. Some of these roads are designated as "Scenic Byways", and have "Points of Interest" and "Scenic Views" at specified points, with pullouts, usually paved, to accomodate curious visitors. Many include fascinating explanations of the geology, how the formations came to be, or identify landmarks on the horizion. I know one in Arizona that locates and identifies over a dozen extinct volcanoes visible from that point. Usually there are alternate routes, not designated "scenic", through much the same landscape, and they are just as scenic, perhaps even more so, but they have fewer specified viewpoints and pullouts.

If you are only going from Here to There, and how quickly you can get there is your only concern, the Interstates are almost always the best choice, but for seeing the sights or learning about the land or just about any other purpose, the common highways are vastly superior to the Interstates, and many, especially the Scenic Byways, are ideal for the casual traveler or newby on the Road.

But there is something even better.

Back Roads

The best roads of all are the Back Roads. They are the least good from the viewpoint of maintenance. Many are not paved. Some are gravel, some are dirt, some are little more than ruts, and are impassable by any vehicle lacking four-wheel-drive. Or possibly a dirt-bike in the hands of a master rider. Those that are paved often need maintenance. Some are so badly out of repair that they would be more usable if they had never been paved at all. Even so, they are generally better than most roads of two or three centuries ago, roads that were called highways. Two hundred years ago, it was common for young fops to bet each other they could drive their carriages to the next town, a matter of twenty miles, without breaking an axle. Sometimes they would win the bet.

But there are far more back roads than highways, and they go to places no other roads can reach. Some are state roads, most are county or local. There are so many of them that the mapping companies cannot keep up; I have avoided a route because it was fifty miles of dirt, then learned it had been paved the previous year. I have also gotten two-thirds of the way down a paved mountain road only to find a bridge had been washed out, and had to turn back. It is usually a good idea to ask the locals before you start.

It is also profitable to discuss the roads with them. There are few, if any, historical markers or labelled points of interest on the back roads, but the locals know. "Yeah, stop right about here and hike mebbe half a mile up the crick. There's a real good waterfall there, flows real strong this time o' year." Or, "I dunno. There's a mighty steep place 'bout twelve miles up. Kinda doubt you kin git your trailer up it." Sure, there are a few who think it mighty funny to mislead the tourist, but the vast majority, if you treat them with respect and do not condescend, will be friendly and helpful.

Natural wonders, spires and arches and balancing rocks and such, were not planned. ("Why", asked the tourist, "did they build the ruins so far from the highway?") They are where they are, and usually there is nothing more than a hiking trail to reach them. Arches National Park was once like that. When Edward Abbott wrote "Let the people walk!", he was objecting to the building of a paved road through the park. He was not, as the Park Service implies today, promoting the hiking trails that have since been laid out. Often, though, you can find a back road that leads, if not to the wonder, at least to within hiking distance. Most of the worthwhile sites (and by "most" I mean a lot more than half) can only be reached this way. Come to think of it, I am not aware of a single Interstate which passes through a National Park or Monument, with the lone exception of I-40 through Petrified Forest National Park. Some come fairly close, but not through. And even on that one, there is nothing worth seeing from the highway.

Read all of the guidebooks, read the tales of travels and adventures and What I Saw, immerse yourself in the internet to dig out all that has been written about things to see, and your list will encompass less than a tenth of what is out here. You can see a lot if you stick to the highways and guidebooks, but the best is tucked away. Even Yellowstone can be beaten, except maybe for Old Faithful. Yosemite's Half Dome is not only not unique, it is nothing special; I have seen a dozen more impressive rocks. The fabulous rocks of Arches pale when compared to the granite fields within a few miles of Vedauwoo, and you can only reach those fields via a back road off of a back road, or by way of another back road off of a different back road. And even then, you will still have to walk.

Of one thing I can assure you: Whatever back roads you explore, you will find them worthwhile. Even if there is nothing unique, you will find, if you look, that each area is different, sometimes subtlely, sometimes dramatically. But possibly the best part is that you never know what you will find around that curve, or on the other side of the mountain, not until you go there and look. The other side is never just like this side.

Two Trails

Experienced hikers can tell you, there are twice as many trails as appear on the maps. The mountain men, and later the settlers and the cowboys, learned this from the Indian. Charles M. Russell, the cowboy artist and story-teller, notes in one of his tales, that he remembered asking an Indian why his people never lost their way. The reply was that a white man only looks straight ahead, and thus sees one side of the trail. The Indian looks in all directions, and sees everything. So every trail is actually two trails, one going out, one coming back. Even a circular trail is two, the one clockwise, and the other counter-clockwise. The two trails are far more distinct than you might think. The back sides of things are often not at all comparable to the front sides. The two sides of a rock may seem to be different rocks altogether. And most of what you see on the way back was hidden behind what you saw on the way out; there could be *anything* there, and usually is.

Many hikers have become lost, even fatally, from failure to look back. They spend half of the day going out, then turn around and come back, or try to. But nothing is familiar. They would swear that *that* rock, *that* tree, *that* cliff, was nowhere near their trail; they have never seen it, or anything like it. So they try another trail And another. They become confused. That is all a confusion is, just too many things happening at once. Next thing you know, they are off somewhere that they really never were, and now they cannot even retrace their route up. Dusk comes and they are still not back, and the emergency rescue teams go find them, hopefully before it is too late.

The trail on the way out winds around a low and dark outcropping. There is nothing distinctive about it, nothing in particular to draw attention. Many people would pay it no mind, might not even notice it. The trail back passes a under a completely different bluff, of a different color and a different shape. It is prominent and unique, ao impossible to miss that I can easily imagine a confused hiker puzzling over where this cliff came from. It is fortunate that there is no other path one can take, for these two bluffs are simply sides of the same rock.

Roads are trails. Highways, even the great Interstates, are still trails. And they, like all other trails, work both ways. South of I-10 in Arizona there lies a mountain. The only thing special about it is that it stands isolated in the low desert. Most such drivers do not even notice it at all. The first time I saw it, I was riding as a passenger in a car. I made a quick sketch when it lay ahead of us. A few minutes later, I did a second, then a third, a fourth, and a fifth as it passed into the distance behind us. If you looked at the five sketches in order, you could perceive they were all of the same peak, but if you scrambled their sequence, or just looked at the first and last, you would find it hard to believe they were the same mountain. Such things are common, if you look for them, and this is on a highway through long, flat, open country. The very same road, passing through the Dome Rock Mountains just east of California, is a twisting corkscrew in three dimensions, left and right and down and up, almost never just one of these at a time. In spite of it being a smooth, well-graded high-speed Interstate (though the speed limit here is only fifty-five, not the seventy-five when it debouches into the flatlands), the curves are still such as to demand attention, especially of overly safety-conscious city dwellers, so much attention that little is left over for the hills amongst which you wander. The situation is made even worse because most of the drivers are doing seventy or more anyway. Take it a little slower! You are not *required* to match the speed limit, just to not exceed it. Slow down. Let the others pass you. Look at something besides the pavement. Brown hills and carved cliffs, unique sculptures by wind and wet, of a type you will find in many places, but also in shapes that exist nowhere else, and may not exist here next year. Pay attention to everything that is there, photograph it in your mind, remember it. Then, when you reach the plain, turn around and do it all over again. You will recognize very little, for the east sides do not resemble the west sides except in broad general. I used helmet cameras to make a video of this very trip, both ways, then edited them to play both recordings on a split screen, but with one running backwards. Sort of seeing both sides at once. Even the Interstates yield multiple views.

Even so, I usually prefer to take the back roads; they tend to be more scenic, and feel more relaxed. Granted, I have the distinct advantage of being on a motorcycle. I am not enclosed in a steel box, with views restricted by the limiting windows, not cut off from the wind and the sounds and the smells of the environment. I do not so much observe as experience; the land is not a thing apart from me. A large part is my own attitude, I am sure, but I feel better, more free, on the back roads. One is not moving so swiftly, often much more slowly; since the faster one is traveling, the more attention must be given to driving, and the more leisurely one is rolling along, the more time one has to observe the surroundings. It is also much easier to stop just to look around; on interstates, it is often illegal to stop at all, except or emergencies. One must wait for rest areas and "points of interest", which are like beliefs: Somebody else's idea of what is worthwhile or interesting. Back roads abound with points of interest, even vast areas of interest. Some of them are marked. There are "historical markers", memorials to significant events of the past. Many are pretty dull: "Coronado passed this way", or "Washington slept here". Others are rather obvious: "Look south for a pretty view". But Historical Markers and Scenic Views are, like "scenic routes", the lesser trails. The greater trails are the views you discover yourself. They are rarely marked, for the locals pay little attention (they see these sights every day; they are nothing unusual, not to them), and the non-locals do not know they are there. But to me they are special. They are beautiful, they are spectacular, they are awesome and wonderful, and unique. Okay, some of them are unmissable, such as Grand Canyon; there is no way one could drive by it and not notice. But there are others; there is a mountain, Shavano, north of route 50 in Colorado. It stands alone in solitary splendor, more isolated than Mount Shasta, a snow-capped peak in the middle of dry desert. It is a landmark; there are even signs pointing out the route to reach it. I will not say you can't miss it, because you *can*; I have met several people who drove right by it and never noticed. Just travel like the white man, only looking straight ahead. Or ride the Indian way, and see the other trail. And the mountain.

Scene:
Mount Shavano

Riding US 50 fifteen miles west of Salida, Colorado, you will pass five miles south of Mount Shavano (SHAH-vah-no), a lone, majestic 14,229-foot mass of bedrock with three snow-capped peaks. If the sky is overcast, you may not notice it at all, or pay it much attention if you do. Under a clear sky, it is striking: The broad, purple mountain is darker than the sky, but the snowcap is as white as the brightest clouds. There is a taller mountain north of it, but only forty feet taller, so Mount Shavano appears to be alone. While reminiscent of the Trois Tetons in Grand Teton National Park, it is bigger, taller, smoother, and snowier. It is well worth going a hundred miles out of your way just to see it.

How They Are

Borders

Borders are funny things. They are of great importance, and are utterly trivial. They are usually invisible and have to be marked by signs such as "Welcome to Someplace Else, exactly the same as Where You Came From, but completely different". Try Four Corners, where Utah, Arizona, New Mexico and Colorado meet. There is a bronze plaque at the exact point in a large circle of concrete, each quarter labelled so you know where you are, all enclosed by a ring of stalls where you can buy souvenirs: Native jewelry, native musical instruments, native T-shirts, and even native rocks. The prices are quite fair, and you don't have to worry about sales tax (which is different in each of the four states), because the whole thing is in a Navajo reservation.

Sometimes the border is a river, which makes it rather obvious, but the land on either side is identical. Except entering Nevada. I recall riding from Arizona, with a couple of small buildings here and there, nothing over fifteen feet tall, and over a bridge, to find myself surrounded by ten-story casinos. Sometimes the border is marked unintentionally, even humorously. The border between Arizona and New Mexico is often quite obvious: One state paves with asphalt, the other with concrete. Back when Oregon required a deposit on aluminum cans and plastic bottles, but California did not yet, the I-5 crossing was marked with litter; in California it was abundant, in Oregon, almost non-existent.

Most of the meanings of borders are of little or no concern. Taxes may be slightly different, road rules may change a bit, the speed limit may go up or down. Sometimes they pretend the time changes. What do you mean, it's an hour later than it was two seconds ago? I'm a camper! It's daytime! Maybe mid-afternoon, but no finer than that. Some meanings are significant. For bikers, it is important to know that California requires you to wear a helmet, but they sort of make up for it by allowing lane-splitting. Also, going from California to Arizona, only buy enough gasoline to reach the border, but stock up on cigarettes. In Arizona, gas goes down two dollars per gallon, but cigarettes cost two dollars a pack more. Of course, by the time you read this, the data may have changed. California loves to enact new laws and pass new restrictions. It is the official State Sport. Well, maybe not *official.*

But the important things change slowly, not at the border. The people are the same, the land is the same, the trees, the birds, the sky, the weather . . . everything that truly matters is all the same. Still, people make a great fuss about borders, even die for them.

Funny things, borders.

Just When You Least Expect It

Memorial Day weekend: The first big camping holiday of the year. Everybody is evacuating the city for the long weekend. Perversely, it is now warm enough to go to the mountains to escape the hundred degree heat of Phoenix and friends. There are many campgrounds within a half-day drive. This is a small one, only nine campsites, and they have all been full since Friday morning. Now and then someone would leave, but their sites would not stand empty for ten minutes before some fortunate newcomer would seize upon it with a joyous cry of relief; "See, I told you we would find a spot!" Every day the latecomers would cruise through the campground, desperately seeking a space, any space, all day and well into the dark. I watch them with pity and with smugness, for I know their ways, and every holiday I see the same parade. I am wise in the lore of campgrounds, and I know one must never arrive on Friday or Saturday, nor on Sunday when Monday is a holiday. On weekends you have maybe one chance in twenty of finding a vacant site, one chance in thirty on holiday weekends. I know better.

Truly is it written, arrogance precedeth a fall.

On Monday they all leave, every one of them, off early on their long drive back to the cities. They may be tyros at mountain timing, they may be foolishly optimistic about what they will find, but they are well aware of the traps of Civilization. They know well that the city freeways will be crowded, growing tighter and tighter and slower and slower till the sun goes down. They strive to arrive as early as they can, to precede the worst of the traffic, and hopefully reach home with enough time to get a hot shower and rest up for work tomorrow. I do not share their rush, for I only require two hours or so to reach my next destination, a fine campground, filled to capacity this morning, the next thing to empty by early afternoon. I pack leisurely, and set off for a quick, smooth and uneventful cruise. The Gods chortle in the high hills.

The highway here is divided, with two lanes on either side. It is only lightly used most of the time; often there is not a single vehicle in sight. Today it is quite busy, for this road; cars and campers every couple of hundred yards or so. Heavy traffic by mountain standards. I join the stream, cruising at the speed limit, and fly to meet my fate. Five miles, four miles, three, two, one...

You see, a couple of miles before the first town, the two lanes become one. Then the divided part ends, and a regular two-lane road runs into town. Some four miles before the narrows, the current stops, and the traffic forms a still pool. We sit a minute, ooze forward for a bit, sit a minute, ooze forward a bit. Bumper to bumper, almost, averaging not five miles per hour. It is not reminiscent of Los Angeles, it is exactly the same, except there are two lanes instead of six, and motorcycles are not allowed to split lanes. The growl is the same, the stench is the same, the hot sun and no breeze is the same. It has been years since I have had to endure this civilized insanity. It is humiliating. I, who know the travel patterns. I, who have never arrived at a full campground (well, there was one time, but that is another story). I, who have lived long in the Wild, who have ridden the back roads, who have avoided the cities as they plague they are. I, who am stuck in a traffic jam, on a heavy, loaded bike, which must be braced and balanced at any speed under two miles per hour, and stopped and started with great care lest I fall beneath the trampling wheels. Even I do not know everything.

At least I know where the bottleneck lies. We will speed up after that. We do. We get up to ten. Seems there is an experimental elk crossing, and the caution lights are flashing. Why, I do not know, for there are no elk present. Well, we get through that and into the town where we gain a second lane and a speed limit of forty-five, which we cannot attain because so many cars are pulling into the gas station, or waiting to pull into the gas station. But past that, we get up to forty, then out of town and up to fifty-five. For one mile. Back to twenty, to ten, to five. We crawl another mile in spite of gaining a third lane, till we reach a set of traffic lights, and two lanes of travelers turn off to join the interstate.

At last, after spending more than two hours to go seventeen miles, I am free. I pass through the town and pull over to have a smoke and meditate upon best-laid plans. Old trickster Coyote had played with me again, but I survived once more, and learned another valuable lesson. That is what he does; he tricks you with a superficially good idea, right into danger. If you survive, you are all the better for it. If you survive. The rest of the trip was wonderful, vastly improved by the immense contrast. Rare cars, cool wind in the clear air, tall ponderosa pines at seven thousand feet. I revelled in the glorious peace, arriving, tired, happy, and two hours late, at an empty campground. It was the finest ride since early last fall.

The River

It was far, far away, in miles, in years, and most especially, in knowledge. I puffed air into a plastic kayak and placed it on the headwater of the Susquehanna River. I loaded my gear, then myself, and set out to have adventures. I knew what I was getting into. I knew what lay ahead. I knew what I was doing. And I was completely wrong.

I do not believe I have ever in my life learned more rapidly than I did those first few weeks. As I drifted down the river,I made many mistakes and repairied the results. By the time I had reached Sayre, Pennsylvania, I had pretty well mastered the basics of downstream travel. Then I headed upstream, for I was bound to the West, and the main body of the river went south. And I learned a whole new body of data while fighting the current, a journey as different from downstream as climbing a hill differs from strolling the level. But I did learn. By the time I portaged to the Allegheny, I was ready. I finally knew, accurately, how to ride a river.

The days were golden. The river passed through virgin forest, mostly, away from the farms and pastures of the Susquehanna. A rare village, rarer town. Sometimes a campground, always with a boat launch ramp. A time or two I stopped in one, enjoying the joke of approaching the entrance from the inside. Inquiring about rates and the presence of showers and laundromat, the puzzled proprietors asked about the whereabouts of my car. "No car. I came by canoe."

The woods were green and lush, the undergrowth thick and tangled. Sometimes the mouth of a tributary was blocked with logs and brush, a clumsy debris dam that would behoove me to get out of the river, force me to unload, walk around, and restow my gear. Sometimes I could ride over the barrier, for the water level was immensely variable. The river could rise fifteen feet or more in just two or three hours, and subside equally quickly; the Eastern version of flash floods. Once I was helped around. I spent several days drifting with the wind along the Allegheny Reservoir. When I spied a likely campsite, I would land and lay out my gear. The weather was clear and dry. The rare rains were short and mild, and I had learned how to stay dry. It was an idyllic time. But then I saw a great barrier looming before me, the concrete mass of the Kinzua Dam. I pulled in to a boat ramp on the lake side, planning how to carry boat and bundles to the downstream side, when a dam employee drove up in a pickup truck. It was one of his duties to watch for boaters and carry their gear around the dam. No charge. And he had a fine time doing it.

I resumed drifting, independent of the wind, the only paddling being the odd stroke to keep aligned with the current. The river took a great curve south, and I became the Hero of the Buckaloons Campground. I stopped for a couple of days, and found there was no firewood available. The campground itself had been picked clean, and the firewood for sale had run out. But on the other side of the river, you could not see the bank for the piled masses of driftwood cluttering the entire shore. I offered a proposal to the other campers, then carried a few to the far bank. With axes and hatchets and saws, they carved the driftwood into five or six foot lengths and loaded them on my canoe. I ferried it to the other side, where others unloaded and chopped the wood into campfire lengths while I went back for another cargo. We must have lugged a cord of wood over, and everyone had proper roaring blazes. And I was fed masses of fried chicken that night, and barbecued ribs the next, with pancakes, bacon and eggs each morning.

What a splendid Spring. I bought a copy of *Huckleberry Finn* and read it on the way. I had read it before, and enjoyed it, but reading the tale while living it was an entirely different affair. Running a trot line for catfish, nabbing a foot-long turtle sunning on a rock in the middle of the stream, imagining itself perfectly safe from any possible danger, picking off squab (rock pigeons, technically) under bridges with a Wrist-Rocket slingshot; I ate well on the bounty of the river. Edible riverine greens, watercress and cattails and such, were abundant. It was easier than hiking, more pleasant than biking. I was kicked back, loafing, seeing everything, feeling the breeze, smelling the flowers and trees, and the river (always the river). It was the finest camping I have ever known, except for two drawbacks, significant ones. First, it could not last forever. I was bound downstream, and eventually I would run out of river. And second, my path was laid before me, and I could not change it. I had to go where the river went. Mostly, this was okay, but there were towns and cities. Towns one might pass fairly quickly, but cities would waste an entire day. I had to get as close as I could and still find a campsite, then start very early and paddle to get through and reach another camp. River traffic was not a problem, as I could go where they could not.

And then the river grew foul. Oily scum adhered to my boat. I could no longer bathe in the river, nor purify the water for drinking. Reluctantly, I left it, shipping my canoe and much gear to my family, and setting off on foot. It had been a grand adventure on the oldest of all roads, but I never did it again; the clean streams are too small for navigating properly.
It is no longer a viable lifestyle, but what a grand way to spend a season!

Hiking

Author's note: This may be the oldest essay I have, its original form dating back to the nineteen-seventies. I have changed, losing the vigor and endurance of youth while gaining the patience and understanding of experience. But the woods have not changed. Nor has the Road.

How long is a road? How steeply does it rise and fall? How swiftly does it twist and wind, meandering through the random terrain? How much is there to see and experience, to feel and hear and smell and know as it carries you along to its end which is also its beginning? There is no single answer to any of these questions, even for a specific road, even for a short stretch. It all depends on you, on which choices you select.

Most important is your state of mind. Are you looking? Are you paying attention, sensing what is there, or are your thoughts miles away, on where you are going to be, or where you once were, or what you would rather do? Or is your mind locked down within your car, conversing with a passenger or listening to some audio recording, with only the smallest bit of attention allowed outside to see the pavement immediately ahead? If so, then the road does not even exist.

Also of great influence is the vehicle by which you travel. A car or truck is a cage which keeps you snug in a comfortable habitat, warmed or cooled to the narrow range which you have persuaded yourself is comfortable. It locks out the smells and sounds, keeps you swimming in your own odors of perfume and after-shave and pseudo-pine-scented cardboard, plus the lingering traces of your last burger and the fries you wanted with that. It barriers the wind, and damps every sound till the rumble of your motor can drown them all. A motorcycle is much better than a cage; you are in the environment, you are part of the environment, exposed to the atmosphere and to the reality in which you ride. It is not perfect; even the quietest pipes still allow the motor to obscure some sounds, and you are exposed to the weather. A little rain is okay, if you are dressed for it. Hail is acceptable, so long as it does not cover the road with marbles. Snow can be bad, and torrential downpour, but those impede almost any vehicle. Bicycles are even better, for they are quiet, and slow, providing you with more time to use noticing the world around you. True, you have to work at it, but that is not a bad thing; it keeps your muscles and heart in tune. And the effects of weather are lessened, for your own speed increases the chill of the air and the impact of the rain, but your speed is far less than that of a motorcycle. Best of all, though, is feet. Hiking the road allows you to see, hear, feel, *absorb* the universe. Little attention is needed for navigating; there is scant chance of losing control and veering off and wrecking, possibly injuring your body, and there is just no possibility of colliding with an animal. Except maybe a bear. You can gaze at the scenery through which you are passing, even look behind (and that is important, for half of the view was hidden when it lay before you). And you can instantly stop, you can pause to drink in a special beauty. You do not have to slow down and pull over, possibly turn around and go back to return to the perfect viewing angle. Yes, it is best to travel on foot. If you can.

That is how I live. Mostly in National Forests, sometimes on BLM or other public land. Now and then (well, *then* and then; it is very rare) I will stay in a developed campground;

sometimes, by sheer necessity when there is too great distance between campsites, in a motel room, but I usually just stop wherever I happen to be when the day is done, or I wander upon a site that is too tempting. A small meadow or a forest spot with no undergrowth, near a stream, but not too close, provides the finest camp possible. Very little is needed: A flat spot for a bed, under a tent if it might rain, a slit trench, well away from water, for a latrine, and a shallow hole in the ground for a campfire, a hole that can be filled in when I leave, so the campsite appears undisturbed. Contrary to popular belief, most of the streams and springs in the forests are clean enough to drink. If there are no farms or factories or dwellings upstream, there is no contamination from fertilizers or wastes. Stagnant water is always dangerous, but a swiftly flowing stream with waterfalls and rapids, or a spring bubbling out of a sandy spot, is almost always safe. After all, the local animals drink it all of their lives, and suffer no harm. Maybe a civilized soul who has never tasted water that was not filtered and chlorinated might get sick; they get diarrhea just from drinking water in a city other than their home. For me, this is sufficient, even ample. I can stay a night, or a week, or a month, as I please. But my feet start to itch; I must move on.

Today, I walk. I have come about twelve miles, which has taken seven hours, but that included a stop in a village where I restocked on rice, dry beans, potatos and onions, and added butter, and a chicken for dinner and breakfast. And an ice cream bar, which was consumed before I got out of the town. My pack is a fair bit heavier than usual, but the weight is not onerous, and I only have to carry it a few more miles. The weather is fine, perhaps a bit warm, and the air is clean. There is some traffic on this road, but in a mile or two, a dirt road will branch off and take me back into the unfrequented forest.

Birds are flitting and singing all around, squirrels are chattering and scolding and dashing off as I approach. Except for a couple who ignore me completely. Rather flat ones, lying on the pavement.

The road is fairly straight, at least to me. From a driver's viewpoint of a car travelling along at forty or fifty miles per hour, it is probably very twisty, but to a three-mile-per-hour foot-slogger, it is different. It is also not very level, or only rarely so. Long uphill slopes, and somewhat shorter downgrades, are the norm. The driver likely would not notice them, for his car would glide over effortlessly in just a few seconds. My legs have to work harder going uphill, and it usually takes a few minutes to reach the top, but the gradients are rather shallow; the climb is not strenuous. Plus, the hills are cloaked in tall, thickly-growing ponderosa pines. They are pouring out fresh oxygen, lightly scented with the true pine aroma. You know, it really does not at all resemble the so called "pine-scented" waxes and cleaners and deodorants that city-folk so eagerly buy. They were told that is what pine smells like, and they believe it. Then they come out here, and complain that the aromas are odd!

The grass is long beside the road, and wildflowers are profuse. Weeds, most people would call them, but while the blossoms are smaller than cultivated flowers, their colors are no less vibrant, and their scents no less intense. The bees and butterflies are not complaining. A little bird, flying so fast I cannot identify it, dodges among the stems and snatches a golden butterfly from the air, then swoops up to a perch where she swallows her snack and sings her victory song, a trilling tune so like the roar of a lion who has pulled down her prey, though the sounds are not at all similar. A doe steps out of the forest and, seeing me approaching, stops right in the middle of the tarmac. She has no following fawn, though in this season she should, perhaps as a consequence of her apparant penchant for standing in the road.

And here is my turnoff. A road of pale tan dirt snakes up into the hills. I know, from my map, that there is a stream with a twenty-foot waterfall about six miles back. There I plan to stay for a week or more, not doing anything in particular. A few short hikes, returning always to base camp. Hours spent watching the waterfall, observing the songbirds and water fauna. Chatting with the fishermen and hikers passing through. Napping and dreaming whenever I please. Gazing at the stars so populous in these dark skies. Eating up the excess weight I just bought, with perhaps a few poached squirrels.

But I still have a couple of hours of hoofing before me. The same forest surrounds me; it is not likely to change much in just a few miles. The trees are individuals, though, each one differing from its neighbors in many details. Here is one with two trunks, the divergence occuring four feet from the ground. There is a similar one, but it could be two trees rooted so close together their bases have apparantly fused into one. One ex-giant has been truncated, the upper half severed, possibly by lightning, but so long ago that no trace of the toppled top remains on the ground. Another tree is perforated, hundreds of half-inch holes hammered into its bark by industrious little woodpeckers, who store acorns in the holes, stocking a larder for the barren winter months. Oh, and look at this! The tree is a tremendous slingshot, the thick main bole straight and true, then abruptly terminating, but with two massive branches emerging from either side, then bending to rise straight up, eight feet apart.

The road is somewhat rutted, with clear wide depressions scoured out by unnumbered wheels scuffing their way up the hill. Rabbits and squirrels are more numerous, and cross the dirt trail fearlessly. Rightly so, it appears, for there is no roadkill here. Except a snake, a rather flat one, twisted into a grotesque ampersand. Slaughtered, murdered, not blindly run over. Some driver saw the creeper, and slammed on the brakes with careful timing, causing the wheels to skid as they passed over the body. It might have survived a mere rolling pressure, for there are soft spots in the dirt, and snakes can withstand a great deal of abuse, but the grinding scrub of an unturning wheel sliding along the dirt and gravel . . . The snake was nearly severed in twain.

Most people drive to a campsite, then spend their vacation hiking the hills and trails, perhaps driving to another a few days later to hike again. They must do so, for their time is limited, they only have a week or two to re-create themselves before they must return to their homes and go back to work. Poor things! I do not suffer under the same constraints; I have all of the time in the world. Instead of driving somewhere to camp and hike, I walk there. Think of driving from the village to my campsite, and compare it to my hike. Ten miles. You might have done it in fifteen minutes, and seen very little, smelled and felt nothing. I spent three or four hours. I was *there*, every foot of the way every second. Few people are free to do the same. Somewhat more people, but still not many, would want to live thus. But I am, and I do. True, it does not seem to contribute anything to Society, to Mankind. But, you know, I think it will, someday, eventually. I do not know how, but I cannot believe that something so free, so beautiful, can be meaningless. I do not know what the meaning is, but when I find it, I will let you know. I promise.

Motorcycles

Prejudice. Bigotry. Fanaticism. Call it what you like, but I find motorcycles more attractive, more pleasing, than any other vehicles. It may be because I ride a bike, but it may instead be the reason I ride. Why does not matter. It is.

Bikes are pretty. There is a clean functionality to them. Every part serves a practical purpose, very few are there just for appearance. Many parts are shiny chrome, but they are not chrome to look pretty, but to preserve the metal. Chrome outlasts paint. Of course, the parts are designed and shaped to look pretty, too, but not overly so. Smooth curves instead of harsh angles, that sort of thing. The parts are functional and also aesthetic, but no parts are only aesthetic and not functional. Bikes are prettier than cars. Actually, cars are rather ugly. Modern cars. Cars back in the '50s were pretty. Their appearance was primarily aesthetic, only yielding to the practical when there was little or no choice. I am not at all certain, as I have never done or observed actual wind-tunnel tests, but modern cars appear to be designed to *look* like they are streamlined, to give the impression of what people *think* is streamlining, but is not actually very effective. Like the "spoilers" on the backs of cars, little wings to hold the rear of the car down and improve traction. They are only effective at speeds over a hundred MPH, and thus of no more practical value than the fins popular in the '50s. I have seen many such devices in the city, I rarely, very rarely, see them in the country. Perhaps they are out of style and no longer being made. Still, streamlining can be effective. I recall riding from Los Angeles to Palm Springs with a stiff tailwind, and back against the same wind. I got fifty MPG going out, thirty coming back.

Some bikes are too loud, some are very quiet. It is a matter of the rider's preferences. I recently heard the roar coming well before the vehicles were in sight. When they came, it was a motorcycle, a second, a third, then the vehicle generating the roar: A pickup truck. Some bikers aver that the loud pipes help make motorists aware of the bike. Could be. I do not think it worthwhile, for one cannot hear much over such a roar. I like a bike that is quiet when I am cruising through the Wilds. If I need to let people know I am there, I use the horn. Not the standard "blip, blip" horn, but the loudest I can find. I once had a horn I made myself, a speaker projecting the sound recorded in a computer chip. The sound of screeching tires in a panic stop. Believe me, *that* attracted attention! And that is what the horn is *for*, right?

Sound is only one part of riding a bike. I can hear the birds, and often the animals, and the deafening *chirr* of the cicadas, in season. Most of these sounds you cannot hear in a car, especially when the windows are closed. Except the cicadas. Deaf people can hear them, or at least feel them, their roar is so loud. But feeling is another aspect: The wind in your face, the smoothness or roughness of the road, the occasional insect. (Do you know how you can recognize a happy biker? By the bugs in his teeth.) It can be a disadvantage, though very rarely. Like the time I flew through a swarm of bees, and had to stop and comb a dozen puzzled buzzers out of my beard, without getting stung. Smell also comes into play, for the woods and the deserts and the foothills and the rivers all have their own smells, some fragrances, a few stenches. I once was climbing from desert to foothills through a long stretch of scrub, a stretch of at least twenty miles. The smells in the air changed every mile or two, usually of spices such as cinnamon or cardamom, some unique and unfamiliar, some chemical odors such as petroleum or creosote, and at one time, of rotting meat. A particular valley, a lush cropland in the midst of arid hills, poured forth aromas of melons and fruits and vegetables. If I had dared to close my eyes, I could easily have believed I was in the produce section of a supermarket. You just do not get these aromas when you are in a car; all you can smell is the car, and possibly your laundry detergent.

Best of all is sight. Sure, you can see from inside a car, but it is more like watching a video than like being there. Your view is framed by the windows and windshield; you cannot see up, or down. On a motorcycle, you are *there*. There is nothing, nothing at all, between you and the view, and there is nothing to limit it or circumscribe your vision. The fact that a bike is easier to control, and thus requires less attention, also contributes. Plus, I and others in the know pass slowly. Speed limit forty-five? We do twenty. Often we pull over and stop, which is also easier on a bike. Sure, it takes twice as long to get there, but if you are in such a hurry, why are you out here? To the man in a rush, the road is a smooth place to drag his car over. To those who appreciate it, the Road is a panorama, a living documentary, unspoiled by someone else's idea of what should interest you. Walking is a good way to view it, for you have long periods to notice more detail. A bicycle is also good, better than a motorcycle if you are physically up to it. A car is acceptable, if you have a convertible with the top down, or better, a Jeep whose windshield can be laid flat and out of your way. Flying over will reveal much that can not be otherwise seen, but the view is very sparse on detail.

All things considered, a motorcycle is the best way to tour the Wilds, except possibly by bicycle.

Which reminds me, one must always be alert for the spontaneous humor which may crop up at any time, and must be ready to take advantage of it. I was casually cruising up a twisty mountain road, when I came up behind a fellow biker, rolling along even more slowly than I was. Just ahead of him there were thirty bicycles in a row, struggling up the slope in a very low gear, and courteously keeping to the side to allow motorized machines to pass. But the biker did not pass; he kept to their speed and followed along, singing cowboy round-up songs. Probably impeding the bicyclists, whose laughter must have interfered with their breathing. I passed the herd, slowly, careful to not interfere. . . except by singing "Git along, little dogies, git along".

Only on a motorcycle could that be done.

Safety Second

I camp on a motorcycle. Carry a bit over a hundred pounds of gear. All the heavy stuff, cast iron cookware, water, tools, is carried low, and the light stuff, sleeping bags, clothes, camp stove, is up top. Only a third of the weight is in eighty percent of the bulk. Looks impressive. Looks like four or five hundred pounds. But it is easier to carry than a passenger would be. Still nineteen out of twenty people I meet on the way, usually when I am departing, tell me "Be safe", "Ride carefully".

I am safe. Reasonably. I ride carefully. Sort of. I almost *always* ride slowly, not for safety, but because I enjoy the scenery. I see so much more at twenty or thirty than at forty-five, especially on twisty mountain roads. I have *time*. On a road through a forest, one rides between solid masses of trees. Frequently a gap in the barrier emerges, and a long view, often over a valley, sometimes across a wild meadow, becomes visible. But only for a brief moment. Eyes glued to the road miss it, may not even see that it is there. Even if it is noticed, at forty or fifty miles per hour, there is no time to slow down, much less stop, and the glimpse of beauty is wasted. I can stop, enjoy it, maybe take a picture or two. It happens to be safer, but that is merely a side benefit, purely of secondary importance. If it was not safer, if it was more dangerous to ride slowly, I would still do it. I see more, feel more, smell more. I am more a part of the environment, I am more free. Besides, I am in no hurry to get somewhere. I already *am* where I want to be. I could rush and get to my destination in two hours instead of three or four. I could spend two hours constantly on the lookout for danger, all of my attention on traffic and the road. "Keep your eyes on the road." "Watch the traffic." "Drive defensively." Get to camp, sit down and unwind for an hour, recovering from the ordeal. Three hours of no fun. But I ride slowly, aware of everything, not just the traffic and the road. I have almost twice the time to react to danger, so I am relaxed, not tense. It sometimes may take me longer to notice a hazard, because that is a truly beautiful cliff over there, but at my low speed, I have enough time to react. And when I finally arrive, it is about the same time the "safe" person has recovered and can start having fun. I don't need to rest. A smoke and a stretch, walk around for a few minutes and I am set. And I had fun for all of those three hours.

Granted, in the cities, the roads are for getting somewhere, and nothing else. But this is not the city. Abandon the city viewpoint when you leave the city. *These* roads are meant for enjoying, for seeing That is why so many are designated as "scenic routes". If I were driving a car instead of riding a bike, I would travel in the same way. This life-style is about having fun, enjoying life, having a good time, doing what you want to do. It is not about being safe. You are not safe, you cannot be safe, you are going to *die*. Guarantee it. You may round the corner and run head-on into a drunk speeder. You may quietly stop breathing in your bed on your hundred-twentieth birthday. You may have a fatal heart attack before you finish reading this essay. I do not know where, when or how, but you *are* going to die. My last words will be something like "Yeah! What a ride!" Most people go out with "Well, at least I won't have to go to work tomorrow".

Freedom first! Safety second. Did you know that all you have to do to turn a free society into a slave society is to push safety in all things? Truth. I wrote a whole essay on just that topic. "Safety First" means "Put on your chains". I would rather be a free man fighting a war than a slave in a nation at peace. (Given my druthers, I would be a free man in a nation at peace.) And though I say "Safety second", I am not saying "No safety". Some safety is sensible. Don't light a campfire in high winds or during extreme fire danger. Look both ways before crossing a road. Don't honk your horn at Hell's Angels. But when safety begins to degrade life, it becomes a bad thing. Yes, you might get attacked by a bear. Don't give up hiking; learn how to behave around bears, and carry pepper spray. Yes, a breakdown in Death Valley in August can kill you. Go there anyway, just make sure your vehicle is in good shape, and take lots of water. Everything is dangerous, but reasonable (minor, not onerous) precautions are normally sufficient. Not always; eventually something is going to kill you no matter what you do. Back in my early twenties, when I knew everything and did not bother to secure my food, a bear invaded my camp. I climbed a tree and survived. Later, when I secured my food my way, not the recommended way, it happened again. Had to kill the bear that time, and barely survived. But I did not quit camping. I learned how to properly secure the camp and how to behave around bears. If I had known enough, I could have walked away softly, abandoning my food, and that poor bear would have survived. *Sensible* safety. A bit less freedom, of course, but stashing food in a tree downwind of the camp means I am free to go camping in the first place.

Learn the precautions for the area you are in. The Forest Service has excellent brochures, free. Bears, cougars, wolves, rattlesnakes, scorpions, bison; they can all hurt you or kill you, but are of no significant danger if you are just a bit careful. Weather, especially in mountains, can change swiftly. Freeze to death in July? It can happen. Read the brochures, carry the proper gear, be prepared. It is not hard, it is not expensive, it does not take a long time. It is also fun. The bear precautions can give you quite an insight into bears, a lot of understanding of how they think, of who they are. The more you know about the Wilds, the more you will enjoy them, and the more they will improve you and your life. Think of the precautions as "good manners in the woods". You don't call a black man "nigger" or a jew "kike"; you don't get between a bear sow and her cub. Same thing. The more you learn the wild, the more you become a part of it, the less you need "precautions"; they just sort of happen, they are behavior that fits the wild society, like riding slowly on mountain roads. Be polite to the wild, and it will be polite to you. You will do as you please, but it will also be what pleases the Wild, because what displeases the wild will displease you. So in the end, these safety rules, these *proper, sensible* rules, do not diminish your freedom, because they open new possibilities that you did not have before. You have more choices, more freedom.

Back roads, mountain roads, tend to be twisty and steep. Going slowly is safer, but since there are more views, and more spectacular ones, it also lets you notice. You will need to pull over frequently, because others who do not know better will stack up behind you; there is often no chance to pass on these roads. Pull over, let them by, and while you are at it, you can look around. You will see so much more than otherwise. Your days will be longer, for they will contain so many more events. You will not be a slave to a clock or a schedule. You will be as free as the wind, as free as the road.

Stay free!

Riding the Wind

Wind affects motorcycles. Cars, too, but I have no first-hand knowledge of that, none to speak of. Wind from the side can force a rider to lean. If it is from the right, it is a good thing, because it makes the tires last longer.   But left or right, it places a distinct strain on your arms: One hand has to push, the other side pull. Not too hard, but over time, muscles become sore. If the wind is gusty, it can make you swerve and drift. If it is strong enough, and you are moving fast enough, it can take you right a cross an entire lane, or even farther. This persuades the wise biker to slow down. A headwind can reduce your mileage, a tailwind will stretch it out. But these are minor effects, objective, mundane, mostly physical. The experienced rider knows how to deal with them, and does not even have to think about it. But the subjective results, how you *feel* about it, well, they can be . . . disturbing.

Head winds,for example. Physically, they are not as bad as cross winds. Say forty miles per hour, steady, strong, from straight ahead. At lower speeds it is only annoying, but once you get up to, say, sixty, well, things change. The world becomes different. Different from itself. You feel the wheels, feel them through your feet, feel them reacting to the road. You hear them. They say "Sixty miles per hour". The wind presses against the windshield, deflects upward, over your head, but there is turbulence under it, turbulence that grows with your speed. From long experience, you recognize it: This is one hundred miles per hour. At that speed, riding can be very dangerous. Things happen fast, so you have to react fast. But things are actually happening at only sixty speed; your reflexes want to respond too fast, too far. Your hands on the grips feel the vibration of the road, but also something else, a twist, a change in pressure when the wind varies, as it will, a few degrees left or right. It is not the sharp, crisp, abrupt jolt that comes from striking a rock or a crack, it is softer, slower, more yielding, but just as strong. And there are gusts in the wind, mostly small ones (usually), but each changes the resistance a bit, a small shift of speed, and the bike speeds or slows with it; your body shifts with it, your butt feels it, feels the body saying "change" while the feet say "steady", and the butt knows not what to think. But then, it rarely does.

And all of these contrary sensations, contradicting signals, adding up to, what? The ride, the world, seems surreal, alien.   The air feels mushy, almost like pushing through molasses. You feel acceleration and deceleration at the same time.   You feel as if you are fighting, struggling to keep some semblance of normality. You cannot smoothly fit to it, because it changes, it does not fit itself. Muscles tense, fighting a thing that does not fight back. You do not fight the wind, you blow right through it. You do not fight the road, for it is smooth and docile. There is nothing to fight, but all of your sensations say there is. It is like a sudden gust, unexpected, that swerves the bike across the lane, but it is steady, constant, you know it is there, always there, you *expect* unexpected gusts. All things are normal, but they are different and incompatible normals, mutually exclusive, yet all present at once. Everything, all of them together, is wrong, impossible, unearthly. Riding at one hundred miles per hour through molasses. Hell.

But the you near your destination and turn. After a few miles you turn again, and now the wind is at your back.

Now it is a tail wind. Forty miles per hour, steady,

strong, from straight behind. Still doing sixty, I float on the air, into a gentle twenty mile per hour breeze that I do not even feel. It is almost nothing, it *is* nothing, in contrast. I am no longer moving, I am standing still, and all else is spinning past. The trees are running on motionless trunks, the rocks roll by without turning over, birds fly backwards, bushes nod with their trotting roots embedded in the soil. Tracer bullets of yellow dashes miss me to the left, zipping along with the swiftly flowing asphalt. My bike is a balloon drifting low over a frantic landscape. I am quiet, calm and serene, as the world rushes by to see where I have been. I carry the bike with me, with effortless ease. The Road stretches on, endless, eternal. I finally reach my destination, but I do not want to stop, for this is the Biker's Heaven.

But I must stop. Sure, I could ride for another ten or fifteen minutes, even another hour. It would be fun, it would be fine. But at the end I would have to stop. I would have to turn around. I would have to fight the head wind for longer than I enjoyed it. Back in medieval times, meals began with the sweet. Today, we save it for dessert. I think we are wise to do so. End on a high note. Always leave them wanting more.

The Road is best when it is like that.

Stagecoach and Bus

Long distance transportation in the early days of the West was by horse, pack mule, wagon and ship. Ships we still use. Pack mules and wagons for freight have been superceded by trucks and trains, and horses and passenger wagons, including carriages, have been replaced by cars, busses and airplanes. But in between the wagons and the busses was the Stagecoach.

Everyone is familiar with the stagecoach of the Old West; we have seen so many in movies and television shows. These coaches themselves are pretty authentic, basically a stout carriage with a bare luggage rack on top and a covered one in back, pulled by four horses. There is another covered rack under the driver's bench, but we never see that used in the movies unless they are pulling out a strongbox for some bandits. But when we see them in motion, invariably they are rolling along at fifteen or twenty miles per hour, or more when they are being chased. And that, I am afraid, was *not* the case. Perhaps when being pursued by a playful band of Indians, or when making a dramatic entrance into a town, but not when just rolling along, covering ground. Sir Richard Francis Burton, explorer of the Nile and translator of *The Thousand Nights and a Night*, also wrote *The City of the Saints and Across the Rocky Mountains to California*. In that book, he recounts his travels by stagecoach in 1860, and included, as an appendix to the book, his itinerary, a sort of diary, including distance traveled and departure and arrival times for each stage station. There were a few exceptional entries, such as one distance of sixteen miles covered in only two hours (eight miles per hour), but the vast majority of the entries for the plains east of Salt Lake City indicate speeds of four to six miles per hour, and for the mountains to the west, only three to five. Two miles per hour is a common walking pace.

Mark Twain, as a teenager, journeyed with his brother from St. Louis, Missouri, to Carson City, Nevada, on a stagecoach, and recounts the journey in his book *Roughing It*. The fare was one hundred fifty dollars. For most of the trip, they were the only two passengers; the rest of the load was mail. As he describes it in his book *Roughing It*:

> We had twenty-seven hundred pounds of it
> aboard, the driver said—"a little for Brigham,
> and Carson, and 'Frisco, but the heft of it for the

> Injuns, which is powerful troublesome 'thout
> they get plenty of truck to read." But as he just
> then got up a fearful convulsion of his
> countenance which was suggestive of a wink
> being swallowed by an earthquake, we guessed
> that his remark was intended to be facetious, and
> to mean that we would unload the most of our
> mail matter somewhere on the Plains and leave it
> to the Indians, or whosoever wanted it.

But, as he described it, the mailbags made a wonderful mattress, and having no ladies along meant they could strip down to their long underwear during the stiflingly hot days.

Mr. Twain notes a particularly fast passage just west of St. Louis, Missouri, when the stagecoach was "spinning along at the rate of eight or ten miles an hour." But that was on the plains, and near to "civilization". Naturally, the farther west one went the coarser the roads became, and once the roads entered the mountains, steep grades became common.

The stagecoaches themselves were simply strongly-built carriages, very similar to coaches used at the time back East and in Europe. The body was, like that of the Conestoga wagon, watertight. When it was necessary to ford a river, the stagecoach would float across; that is why the front and rear bottoms were curved; the streamlining was like a boat hull, for easier passage through the water. In some western movies, such as *Stagecoach*, logs were tied to the sides for flotation. I would not say that was never done, but it was usually not needed. Modern busses have no such feature, but then, they do not need it. The brakes were simple and reliable. In the photograph above, you can see a rectanguar block just in front of the rear wheel. That is the brake shoe. The driver pulled a lever, which pressed the shoes against the iron tires of the rear wheels, and the friction slowed and stopped the coach. Modern brakes on busses and cars are still basically the same, except the brake shoes press on the wheel rims instead of the tires. The turning radius was pretty large, because the entire front axle swivelled, not just the wheels, as is done today. Bigger wheels can pass over rocks and other obstructions more easily than small wheels, so the wheels were as large as it was practical to make them. But the front wheels could only turn so far before touching the body, and that is why the front wheels are smaller than the rear ones, so they can turn farther. Iron or steel springs had been in use for over a century, but they were uncomfortable and did not last very long; they were quite unsuitable for the rough western roads. In 1827 the Abbot-Downing Company of Concord, New Hampshire, developed the Concord Stagecoach. Instead of metal springs, the carriage body was suspended on long leather straps that ran from the front to the back. These absorbed shocks and imparted a swinging motion which caused Mark Twain to compare the coach to "a cradle on wheels". They outlasted the metal springs, and were a lot easier and cheaper to replace.

Here is a copy of Stagecoach Rules. I do not know which route or stage company they were for, nor the year they were used, but they are authentic, and quite typical of every major stage line in the 1800s:

1. Abstinence from liquor is requested, but if you must drink, share the bottle. To do otherwise makes you appear selfish and unneighborly.
2. If ladies are present, gentlemen are urged to forego smoking cigars and pipes as the odor of the same is repugnant to the Gentle Sex. Chewing tobacco is permitted, but spit WITH the wind, not against it.

3. Gentlemen must refrain from the use of rough language in the presence of Ladies and Children.
4. Buffalo robes are provided for your comfort during the cold weather. Hogging robes will not be tolerated and the offender will be made to ride with the driver.
5. Don't snore loudly while sleeping or use a fellow passenger's shoulder for a pillow; he (or she) may not understand and friction may result.
6. Firearms may be kept on your person for use in emergencies. Do not fire them for pleasure or shoot at wild animals as the sound riles the horses.
7. In the event of runaway horses, remain calm. Leaping from the coach in panic will leave you injured, at the mercy of the elements, hostile Indians and hungry coyotes.
8. Forbidden topics of conversation are Stagecoach robberies and Indian uprisings.
9. Gents guilty of unchivalrous behavior toward Lady passengers will be put off the stage. It's a long walk back. A word to the Wise is sufficient.

By way of comparison, I looked up the modern rules for interstate bus lines. These rules were posted on one line's website:

Please stay in your seat while the bus is moving. When we say 'enjoy your trip' we don't mean rolling half way down the bus if it needs to stop quickly.

There's no smoking allowed on the bus (it's against federal law). But don't worry, our buses stop about every two hours so you can have a smoke outside.

Please don't take photos, video or make audio recordings of [our] staff, equipment or procedures (most of us haven't been to acting school and just want to do our jobs).

Absolutely no alcohol, drugs or weapons anywhere on the bus (including in your checked baggage).

This is a stickler for us – no unruly behavior on the bus. No shouting, being loud, or generally disturbing the driver or other passengers. Just chill out, be nice and enjoy the ride.

We don't let animals on board .... The only exception is legitimate service animals riding together with a disabled person. For more information, see our Customers with Disabilities page.

At first reading, the rules are quite different, but on closer examination, you can see how the rules have evolved as Society has slipped away from Liberty. You cannot smoke, even if no one objects. "Do not bother the ladies" has become "Be quiet! Do not do anything that even *might* disturb anyone." "Share your liquor" has become "No liquor." And as for weapons, why, the stagecoach folk would not even dream of disallowing a gun, but today, so cowardly and fearful are the politicians, they will not even allow a pistol packed away in stored baggage!

The railroads drastically impacted stagecoach use, but never completely replaced it; there still were, and are, places with no rail service. But the motorized bus and the greatly improved roads eventually replaced the last coaches. Today, the stagecoach is only a part of history.

But the fare from St. Louis to Virginia City is still about one hundred fifty dollars.

Who They Are

Angeles Crest Highway

I lived in Los Angeles for many years. One of the things that made it tolerable was the Angeles National Forest. Sixteen to twenty miles from my home (for I did move on occasion) was the border of the forest, and right through the middle, for forty miles, ran California Route 2, the Angeles Crest Highway. The terrain varied from desert scrub and rough canyons to rich pine forest in pleasant valleys to bare snow-capped peaks. There were plenty of campgrounds, and even more good dispersed spots all along the highway. I could leave work on a Friday, change clothes and grab my prepacked camping gear, and reach my campsite in about an hour. On Monday morning, I could break camp, head home, shower and change, and be at work on time. I did this many, many times.

One of my favorite sites lay on the branch road that led to Mount Wilson Observatory. I called it Squirrel Hill, after the multitude of squirrels and chipmunks who played across the rock face each morning, frisking and revelling in the warm morning sun. It also bore a steep switchback trail leading to a high crest above. Since it was not a developed campground, I could never have a campfire, nor could I leave gear unattended for long

because it was a very popular trailhead. Even so, it offered a fine view, and was a good place to be out of the city.

The old Observatory complex at the end of that road was another good place to visit. There were good trails in wide open forest, museum displays of the history of the observatory, and a direct view to the west of the top of a thick brown cloud that almost always overlay Los Angeles. Often I would leave the city on a clear and cloudless day, ride to Mount Wilson, and be unable to see the slightest trace of the buildings a mile below. A mile or so short of the peak was a large parking area with a stupendous and dizzying view of a vegetation clad canyon, and the head of an old trail that even had a couple of tunnels. It was popular for bicycles.

The Observatory Road turned off from the Angeles Crest Highway just a short way past the Angeles Highway turnoff, at the Red Box picnic area. There were a couple of trailheads here which led to several walk-in campgrounds, good hikes on intermediate to difficult trails. Also located at Red Box was the Haramokngna American Indian Cultural Center, with a small but very informative museum. There is a small plain just north of and visible from Red Box, which was where the local tribes would meet when they came up to harvest acorns and such, and took the opportunity to trade with each other. "Haramokngna" means "The Place Where People Meet".

Halfway to Red Box was the Switzer Creek Picnic Area. It was down a steep winding road, a bit daunting, especially when going up, because there were a couple of blind turns, and you never knew what oncoming traffic there might be. But once you got there it was very pleasant. There was no camping allowed, or overnight parking, but it had at least a dozen picnic sites with tables and fire grills. Following down the creek was an easy forest trail. There were several more picnic sites along it, some of which had been used as campsites. I do not know if it was allowed or not, but clearly, hikers had walked in and used them. This was one of the wettest areas in the Angeles Forest, and it usually was quite cool. The hike was not at all strenuous, but it did cross the creek a couple of times, so you were likely to get your feet wet, even with the creek as low as it was. By the way, this is all past tense because I have not been back there for years. Who knows what the Californians may have changed? President Obama, when he was signing the proclamation to change the forest to a National Monument, said there would be no changes to the hiking and camping, but that was a political promise. You know what they are worth.

Off another branch road, the Angeles Highway, lay my favorite campground, named Monte Cristo, after a nearby mine. It was not spectacular, but it had everything necessary: Water, toilets, firewood, and space. It was central to several trails, and bore wooded cliffs on one side, and rocky arroyos on the other. It was quiet and peaceful. Its only drawback was its popularity; every campground in the forest was heavily used, there being so many people living within easy reach of them.

The Angeles Crest Highway was very popular among motorcyclists. Many went there, as I did, for a pleasant ride in cool, open, relatively clean air. Others were thrill seekers. They would come dashing along on their shiny sports bikes, wearing full racing gear, and ignoring speed limits. They wanted the experience of running winding roads at high speed. Rather foolish, I always thought, for I saw many paramedics and wreckers hauling up the remnants of bikes, and of bikers. Now, I can ride the hairpin-cornered roads, but I do it slowly. It is not that I fear losing control or dropping the bike; it is the cars driven by relatively inexperienced people, the ones who drift across the center line, and who panic or freeze if they see an oncoming bike. The cars could be even worse than the bikes; I almost never rode this highway after dark, partly because there is a nut-group who vie for seeing who can run the Angeles Crest the fastest, after dark, with no lights. Again, it is probably because Los Angeles is so close; cities seem to breed insanity.

Bicyclists were also common. Some of them rode all the way up, then coasted down, a long, hard day of good exercise and exhilarating fun. Others were driven up by a friend and dropped off with their machine. There were several firms offering the service of hauling bicycles to the observatory, where they would rent them out. The renters would get all of the fun of the long coast down without the strenuous task of riding up. Having your cake, and eating it, too. For a price.

The best part of the highway is the lower part. There is more vegetation, and more variety of views. But the upper parts are still very good, for you can often see much, much farther, you get up among cool nine-thousand-foot peaks, and there are fewer people. It is less than fifty miles from one end to the other, so it makes for a nice day trip, casually driving far up, having a leisurely lunch, and sedately riding back.

The forest, as I knew it, has changed mightily; it suffered a devastating burn, was replanted (stupidly) with greasewood, and most was renamed the San Gabriel Mountains National Monument. Time has also worn away at it, largely due to the ongoing drought. One of the day attractions I mentioned before is Switzer Creek and Switzer Falls. When I first moved to Los Angeles, Switzer Creek was fifteen feet wide. By the time I left, I could step over it without wetting my shoes, and the Falls were reduced to a dribble.

I have many pleasant memories of the Crest Highway, and am glad it was there, but I cannot honestly say I miss it. Every thing it has I have found elsewhere, and of higher quality.

But the Angeles Crest Highway kept me reminded of what I was working for, of the Home to which I have since returned. For that, I shall always be grateful.

Scene: San Jacinto Mountains

It may be you live in the Southern California megalopolis. You read this book, perhaps, and yearn to be here. But you have duties, and can only afford a weekend. Well, there is hope.

From downtown Los Angeles to Palm Desert is about one hundred twenty miles, two hours, with good traffic (hah!), and less from San Diego. Some ten miles south on Route 74 will take you to Pinyon Flat, spiritually and scenically about as far from LA as you can get. The Road runs straight and true for a few miles, then begins to wind, and climb. Broad loops, sharp turns, always up, till you rise above the smog. The folks in Palm Desert will deny it, but they do have smog, thin by Los Angeles standards, foul compared to the Wilds. There is a fine overlook. In one direction, you look down on what you are escaping; in the other, the Wilds.

It is a beautiful place, an almost perfect gateway to a small piece of the Wild.

Pinyon Flats

Ride south from the town of Palm Desert. Rising from the open plains, a long straight incline introduces you to the hills. The road succumbs to the contours and winds upward into the mountains where it must twist and turn and cling precariously to the cliffs. The land is dry, no humidity at all, but the flora is almost lush. Three thousand feet above the desert, only twelve miles from the sprawl called a city, lies a whole other world.

The highway is lightly traveled, for Southern California. Half a mile north of it lies the campground. The campground is beautiful, and wild, and has water. Late April is the best time to visit, just after the wet and before the heat. But be warned: The winds can be fierce! The prevailing sea breeze funnels through a low point in the mountain range, concentrating its energy into a narrow gap, and you are sitting right smack dab in the middle of it. The campground is not too small, some twenty sites or so, but they lie spread well apart. Many trees, Pinyon Pines, stand in and around the campground and beyond, old trees, a century or two, some much more, but small, few over twenty feet tall, for this is an arid land, and they grow so slowly. But it has been a wet winter. It is now early April, and the rains shall fall no more this year, though their sign is still present. The road is dirt, not even gravelled. It is creased like corduroy with ruts six or eight inches deep. Last week it was mud; today it is dry, and rock hard. Traversing this road is difficult for a car, and barely possible for a motorcycle. The forest service will bring in a grader and level it off before the camping season takes off. Maybe around the first week of May. Grass is green, and long. Cactus is plump. Scrub that always looks dead and sere to visitors from kinder environs is draped with miniscule newborn leaves, leaves that will linger for only a few weeks, desperately storing enough energy to sustain the roots till the rains return.

Many trails wind through the remnant forest which is the Flats, and they are the primary reason to come here. Brightly colored desert wildflowers are ubiquitous, miniature blossoms each smaller than a fingernail, frantically breeding a new crop of seeds, to be scattered in the  sure and certain hope that maybe, someday, a few of them may escape the notice of the birds and germinate to preserve the species for one more generation. They cover the ground as a short-nap carpet. A rather threadbare carpet, for they "cover the ground" by desert standards. Much bare dirt is still visible.

Every cactus blooms, in waxy red and orange and yellow, and purple and blue, four- and five-inch shouts of brilliance against the gray and green. Life is in riot, a silent cacophony of urgent growth, a desperate determined scramble for whatever it can get during this brief moment of clement conditions. Two weeks ago, it was wet and freezing; two weeks from now it will be dry and searing. Now is a touch, a hint, a remembrance of Eden.

Beyond the campground lies all that remains of Pinyon Flats. It once comprised this entire plateau, ten or fifteen miles in all directions. Now it is reduced to barely a single square mile, bounded by paved roads, bordered by pasture. But within that square mile, it survives, protected, cherished by Man who, fortunately, realized the beauty before it was too late, before it had all been sequestered for practical purposes.

Pinyon pines cluster as closely as they will anywhere, often even touching their neighbors. Ancient Grandfathers, hundreds of years old, but short and compact, the Bushmen of this western Kalihari, watch over their teeming descendants. Like the Kalihari, Pinyon Flats is not what it seems. It is a forest that does not look like a forest. The trees are too short, often appearing to be mere shrubs. There is little undergrowth, and that is largely cactus. It fools the unwary, the tenderfoot, the town dweller who knows only parks and boulevards. He walks into this desert, this "flat", innocent, suspecting nothing. He admires the gnarled tree, smiles at the spread of flowers, smugly avoids the cluster of cactus, looks around . . . . and suddenly realizes he is lost.

He has no idea in which direction lies the campsite, for there are no landmarks. These trees are diminutive, yet still tall enough to hide the distant high peaks, and the sun is no help, for he did not note if he set out north, east, south or west. The ground is loose fine  gravel and coarse sand, dry and tightly packed, and is incapable of holding footprints. Not footprints *he* could recognize. The groundcover is so sparse, not one step in ten has bent a stem. The bushes are far enough apart that he has brushed against none of them, broken no twigs, left no trace upon them. He has left no trail, no sign at all; at least, none that he can read. Lost! And he thought he had walked no more than a hundred yards.

Pinyon Flats is playing a joke. He *is* within a hundred yards of his camp. If he picks the correct direction, he could be back in just a few seconds. But if he selects any direction, and holds true to that line, then in no more than a mile, and likely half that, he will come across a trail, which will surely lead him somewhere. And even if he finds no trail, he will soon see a paved road. He knows roads; he can easily find his way on them. But he is not aware of this, for his experience includes nothing comparable, and so he is lost.

The one who knows directions, who can read sky and shadow, roams unconcerned, directing all of his attention to the bounding and unbounded beauty. He knows where he is. Even under a full overcast, there are many gaps between the trees. A stroll of just a rod or two will give him a glimpse of the ranges of mountains surrounding the valley, ranges with distinctive skylines. If you examine them before starting on your hike, you will be able to tell your direction at any time with certainty, and know the direct route back to camp.

Dead and down wood is abundant, and gathering it for firewood is allowed. Every day on my frequent walks through the endless assortment of possible paths, I would pick up a shoulder-load of long branches just before arriving back at camp. By the time I left, there must have been a weeks worth of excess wood, left for the next tenant. Of course, much of it remained because half of the time the wind was too strong to allow a safe campfire. And beside the downed dead wood, there were so many fascinating sights to see in this "dead" land.

A grove of prickly pear eight and ten feet wide radiates from the ruin of an ancient ancestor, the forefather who first rooted here a century or more ago, who seeded in a circle a new generation, who spread their own descendants farther and farther still.

A snake slithers through, fleeing the footsteps he hears with his belly. A small rabbit crouches in shadow, trembling at the presence of a new predator, not believing that this two-leg is harmless, for to him, any creature larger than himself is a mortal danger, and even smaller ones are worth wariness. He trembles, his fear builds, he twitches, he panics, breaks, sprints for a not-distant sanctuary, stops, stares, searches for whatever new dangers lie concealed and biding their time. Fear is a way of life, is *the* way of life, if the rabbit is to survive.

The flowers tend to crowd, to cluster, to congregate, but the bushes stand aloof, maintaining a measured distance from each comrade, greedily grasping every precious morsel of rare water. The pines are even less sociable, their roots long arms to hold their relatives at length. In the areas near their trunks they confiscate even the surface moisture, forcing the brush to

keep its distance. Farther off, deep roots hoard every drop, thus allowing the organism to remain green, or at least gray-green, when all of the smaller plants must feign death as they hibernate, not through winter, but through summer and fall, the times of drought. And so many, so very very many, succumb. Their child mortality is terrifying, their infant mortality almost infinite. But those who survive, those few who survive, do survive, for years, decades, centuries. They are the natural bonsai, bushes a foot high and a century old, gnarled and twisted, weathered and worn, rough, tough, tough enough to endure years of famine, years of the barest, most minimal subsistence, tough enough.

But enough is not always enough. Most never germinate, most who do never know the next rain, most expire in a year, or a decade. And even the toughest, the strongest, the luckiest, eventually fail. Perhaps they grow too well, too tall, and a gale overmatches their strength. Perhaps their luck runs out, and a bolt of lighting shatters the trunk, or opens a wound allowing entry to the boring insects or insidious disease. Eventually, the tree falls. Insects will feed on the helpless hulk, and birds will feed on the insects. Dry lichens and fungi and wood-eating microbes devour the stored sunlight, and slowly, very slowly, the moldering corpse returns to sand, aiding another to sprout in its stead, a thousand years after the fallen giant's story began.

And this forest that does not look like a forest persists. It changes constantly, and never changes at all. The timid rabbit hides and flees and feeds and breeds in a doomed struggle to stay alive, and loses the struggle, but wins in the long run, in the inextinguishable flow of kittens, who will struggle and die, but first kindle another link in the long chain of rabbitkind. The scruffy scrub will grow and die, and a very, very few of its seeds will carry on forever. And the forest will look the same, differing only in details, until the climate changes and the long rains return. The pinyon pines will recede, replaced by others,

perhaps by ponderosa, or fir, or aspen, or oak, trees not so tough, not so frugal, trees that know how to use the plentiful water to rapidly rise and shade out the miserly scruffy pinyon. And Pinyon Flats may become Aspen Flats or Oak Flats . . . until the drought returns, the Bad Times for many, the Good Times for the pinyon. Thus the forest will change, and change again, and again, and again, forever and forever. But the Forest will persist. Forever.

Scene:
Ciriaco Summit

It is quite a trip from Los Angeles to Arizona, roughly two hundred fifty miles. It is also one of those roads that is boring except for one or two Scenes. Unless, of course, you *like* passing through endless built-up areas. There is a huge wind farm just west of Palm Springs, which I find quite fascinating. (I know some eco-simps who oppose windmill generators, because some birds have been killed by them. I swear, some of these jerks are only interested in stopping things, and do not much care what it is they stop.) There is the road up to Pinyon Flat, and some forty miles later, the entrance to Joshua Tree National Park. After that, pretty much nothing but open desert for the last hundred miles. Except, five miles past Joshua Tree, Ciriaco Summit: A fuel stop, a grocery store, and a museum.

In the early days of World War Two, the US Army was preparing to invade Africa. The troops, especially the Tankers, had to learn about desert maneuvers. The training ground selected was that last hundred miles, and the man put in charge was General Patton. Here, at Ciriaco Summit, is the George S. Patton Museum. It is surrounded by a selection of tanks and desert vehicles. Inside is a fine collection of weapons and equipment used in the desert warfare, and a beautiful relief map of the entire training area. It has a book store/gift shop, where I found a volume about Patton and his campaigns, written by, of all things, the generals who fought against him.

If you are at all interested in Patton, tanks, or the desert campaigns, this museum is a must-see. Admission is only five dollars, and well worth it.

Arizona 88

This is a short road, barely thirty-six miles, but I know many roads hundreds of miles long which contain less beauty, less interest, less *character.* Yes, that is the right word: Arizona Route 88 is a character.

It begins in Apache Junction, about the most out-lying of the sub-cities that surround Phoenix. It runs northeast to the storied village of Tortilla Flats, from which the Outcasts came. I was bound for Tortilla Campground, quite tired and ready to rest, only to find that the campground had closed for the season on April fifteenth. I arrived on the twentieth. Having little choice, I continued a few miles to a trailhead with a wide parking area (unpaved) and set up a dispersed camp. Dry, of course, but with a set of port-a-potties which precluded the need of digging a cathole. Also heavily infested with gnats, not stinging or biting, but so numerous, you could hardly take a breath without inhaling a couple. My tent had a screen, and I had a headnet to fit over my hat, so the situation was better than tolerable. A Ranger stopped by to check me out, laughed when I explained that I had not known Tortilla Flats was closed, and so was outcast here, and wished me a good night, but warned me campfires were not allowed.

I resumed the next morning, taking it slowly, because the road did wind so, and the scenery was spectacular. Soon I slowed even more, because the road, paved on my map, was not paved on the ground. It was not badly rutted, nor narrowed by rockslides, so clearly some maintenance was done. Skilled maintenance, too, for there was no washboarding such as you get when a grader impatiently drives too fast. The surface was actually quite good for a dirt road, especially for one that twists and writhes along a hillside, later a cliffside when it entered the canyons, dry tributaries of the Gila River. Good, though, is a relative thing. You do not need four-wheel drive, but you do need good suspension and a reasonably high clearance. I, on a motorcycle, was jolted fairly constantly, and somewhere along that road, I have no idea when or where, my horn fell off. My beautiful, self-made bike horn that blared out the squeal of tires locked in a panic stop. Good attention-getter. It is not a good road for most RVs; considering the hairpin turns and single-lane bridges, of which the road boasts several, I doubt one could manage more than a twenty-foot trailer.

The farther I went, the more rugged the land became. Ragged cliffs drew steeper and closer, the sky grew narrower and bluer, and the vegetation, oddly, thicker. After a few miles of rapid reversals (I generally had no idea of what the compass

direction might be), the canyon ended, the walls withdrew, and the road entered the true valley of the Gila.

It was the valley of the Gila River, and I suppose it still is, but there is no longer any Gila River here. Instead, there is Apache Lake lying between Theodore Roosevelt Dam and Horse Mesa Dam. The lake is long and narrow, less than a mile wide, and quite popular among Phoenix folk for boating and fishing. Many of them store their boats in a large marina, rather than trailer them in. Access is much easier if you enter

from the East. You can easily drive in a fifty or sixty foot motor home or fifth-wheel. Of course, you do have to go an extra hundred miles or so, if coming from the West.

When you first see Apache Lake from Route 88, you are already two-thirds of the way up it, for the lake bends north at this point, flowing away from your road. Eventually, if you are wise enough to look back, you will see much of the rest of the lake, and Horse Mesa, for which the Lake's dam is named.

The vegetation is typical of arid desert, but plentiful. Though the lake is still a couple of miles away, evaporation raises the humidity far beyond what a desert would normally display. Saguaro stand as thickly as in their National Park. Chaparral, mesquite and sagebrush grow in thickets so dense you cannot walk through them, not without great effort and even greater destruction.

But carry on a while. Shortly, about the thirty-second mile, you find Burnt Corral Campground. It is quite large, has water and vault toilets, picnic tables, ramadas at many sites, and lies on the shore of the lake. Although the road in, including the four remaining miles to the end of Route 88, is dirt, from the moment you turn off the road, the campground drives are paved. The campground is well-shaded and, lying at nineteen hundred feet, not too cold in Winter. In Spring, it is near perfect, and in Summer, quite tolerable if you have an RV. During the hot weather, campers are allowed to run generators all night long, to power their air conditioners.

Wildlife is abundant, especially birds. There are water snakes in and around the lake, non-venomous, and king snakes, who keep rattlesnakes away. There is a large population of cardinals, and of vultures, and there are a few great blue herons, and sometimes German frauleins.

At the end of the road lies Theodore Roosevelt Lake, offering nothing much more than Burnt Corral, except better sailing on a much wider lake. The campgrounds are pitiful by comparison. A few miles south is the Tonto National Monument, featuring a small cluster of well-preserved cliff dwellings, and offering guided tours, and well worth a visit.

There is so much more to Arizona 88 than I can describe, or even mention, in a single short article. If you look, you are very likely to spot gila monsters. Coyotes, of course, and javelinas. Abundant wildflowers and plentiful cactus blossoms, in the right season. There are many places on the road, narrow as it is, where you can pull over and just look, just be there for an hour or two. If you come in from the West (which I recommend, if you can) best plan on taking all day to do the thirty miles. This is no road to rush upon. Take it leisurely, and it will reward you immensely.

Scene:
Theodore Roosevelt Lake

Almost all lakes and reservoirs that were created by damming a river share much the same shape: A long, more-or-less narrow body, with a dam at one end. TR Lake has the shape, but it is a Pushme-Pullyu, with two headwaters. It swells from Tonto Creek in the West and from Salt River in the East, with the dam smack dab in the middle, on the southwest shore. The lake runs about fifteen miles long and three wide, depending on last season's rainfall, and offers good fishing and good boating, including sailing. Camping is so-so, especially if you tent, because the lake lies in the Tonto Basin of Arizona; only a couple thousand feet elevation, no shade to speak of, very hot in Summer. But they will let you run your generator all night, for air conditioners.

Right at the outlet, just before the dam, stands The Bridge. It is a single simple arch, no frills, nothing fancy, and that is its great beauty: It is pure Bridge.

Scene:
Tonto National Monument

The Indians who lived in the Tonto Basin ever so long ago were no fools, in spite of where they lived (the name "Tonto" means "fool"). They built their homes in caves far up the cliff sides, well out of most weather, and difficult for enemies to reach. The ruins are mostly very well preserved, hardly ruins at all. There is a fine museum, an easy path to the cave, and guided tours. The staff are friendly, with good senses of humor. I heard them discussing questions by foolish tourists, so I asked them why the Indians had built so far from the lake. It took them a few seconds to catch on, but then we had a good laugh.

Salt River Canyon

Burnt Corral in the Tonto Basin is an excellent Spring campground. When it is getting too hot, I like to move to Upper Tonto Creek, some three thousand feet higher, or if it is getting *really* hot, to Winn, in the White Mountains, at nine thousand feet. This is Arizona; figure five degrees temperature drop per thousand feet of altitude increase. Fahrenheit; we Americans are a bit primitive. A thirty-five degree difference as opposed to fifteen degrees makes Winn the less likely choice, but there is another factor, and that is US Route 60.

Route 60 actually runs coast to coast, from Los Angeles to Virginia Beach. The part I am referring to is the seventy-eight mile stretch from Globe to Show Low. It, like over half of the highways in Arizona, is an official Scenic Route. Half of the other ones should be, too. The first thirty miles lies in mountainous woods, part of the Tonto National Forest. Along the way is Jones' Water, a primitive twelve-site campground with tables, firepits, outhouses, and trash disposal, but, in spite of the name, no water. No reservations, either, or fee. But it is very pretty, very quiet, and very dark. I usually stop there for a day or two, even if I have only been on the road for an hour.

A few miles north of Jones' Water, the real fun begins. It is a short stretch, three or four miles, of spectacle. It is the Salt River Canyon. This is rough country. It is not as big as Grand Canyon, not by a long shot, but it is just as rough, and you get to drive right through it. The speed limit drops as low as twenty-five, and not for any bureaucratic reasons; only a fool will speed on this road. I said the land is *rough.* It is like . . . Well, let me put it this way: This is the land that the government gave the Apaches for their reservation.

Got it?

And therein lies the beauty. There are rocks here that were  at one time a single solid spur of bedrock, but have been cracked and shattered by many years of expanding ice into a hundred smaller stones. Their edges have been smoothed and rounded by wind-blown sand and gnawing lichen. And yet, they still stand, a pile of rocks fitted together as if by a master stonemason.

Imagine Grand Canyon with vegetation, pallid greens sprouting from pale red rock walls. That is Salt River Canyon.

There really is a river down there. You can not see it often, but it is there. As the Colorado River has done in Grand Canyon, the Salt River has meandered miles to either side over the ages, slowly, patiently cutting and grinding and carving its bed, sometimes undercutting a towering cliff till it cut too far and caused gargantuan landslides that dammed the river and forced it to take a new path. Multiple levels of vertical cliffs separated by narrow terraces clogged with steep talus slopes climb up and up rounded remnants of hills, quietly awaiting their inevitable destruction. It may be hard to envision, and even harder to believe, but all of this land, all of this unmappable crazy quilt of cliffs and ravines and peaks was once a flat, level, smooth plateau. And water, just water, has wrought this masterpiece sculpture.

Sometime, far in the future, when Mankind has long gone to the galaxy or to the grave, the water's work will be finished. Someday these canyons will be smoother and softer than the Appalachians are today. Someday these lands will be as flat as Kansas, and all of the majesty and awe will have washed away with the silt that the mountains have become. But until then, we have the Canyon. And you really should go see it, before it is too late.

New Mexico 185

It is not a long road at all, just fifty-eight miles. But when it comes to landscape, I know of no more varied route, no trail that passes through so many different scenes, much less in so short a distance.

You start out from Las Cruces, The landscape is urban. Not towering skyscrapers, just buildings, rarely more than a few stories, but lots of them, crammed together because every square foot of land is precious. Or at least expensive. But it swiftly changes to small-town, then suburban. Not your usual suburban, no tract houses, not even much in the way of lawns. Water is precious, here, for even though the city lies right on the Rio Grande, there is a claim on every drop of its water. All along its length, someone has dibs on a certain amount. This is farm country. There are a few cattle, some vegetable fields, but the vast majority is used to grow chile peppers and pecans. It seems an odd combination, but the climate is perfect for both, and out here, Nature sets the ground rules. So instead of lawns, many local folks plant pecan trees Not all of them, but enough live in groves to make it strikingly apparant. Almost as striking as the array of rugged, jagged mountains that line the horizon.

The suburban feel evaporates as you approach the first pecan orchards. Or maybe groves. "Orchard" seems more

appropriate for fruit trees than for nuts. Regardless, the road passes through acres and acres of pecan trees, carefully laid out in serried ranks, orderly rows and columns, in wide, flat fields. Very flat, for the trees are watered by flooding the fields. The care taken in laying them out is obvious when you see flooded fields, every bit under water, but barely an inch or two deep. Many are flooded now, but only accidentally; there was a remarkably heavy rain, up to almost four inches in some areas, which is close to a quarter of the annual allotment, and the water has not yet seeped in. The leaves are just beginning to change, and the farmers (ranchers? grovers?) are anxiously awaiting the first hard freeze. That is when the leaves will fall and get swept away. Then the harvesters come out with their peculiar machines that grasp the branches and shake the trees, shaking loose the tons and tons of nuts. When they are done, the suction machines follow and sweep up the bounty. It seems such a peculiar way to harvest: Vacuum clean the groves, then shake the trees, then vacuum up the nuts. But it works, and works well.

The road winds through mile after mile of pecan groves. Pecans are a major crop around here, probably second only to chile peppers. It is an odd combination. I wonder if anyone makes pecans coated with chiles. But soon bare fields begin to appear, interspersed among the pecan groves. Barren brown dirt, with not a single plant visible. A month ago they were thick with lush green plants, but the plants are gone. They were the big crop, the famous crop, the very symbol of New Mexico: The Chile Pepper. All harvested, the forlorn fields

stripped naked, left to wait, to sleep, till the spring planting time. The annual Hatch Chile Pepper Festival is over, a few fresh chiles shipped around the world, some processed and preserved as salsas and canned peppers, most dried and sent off to be ground into precious chile powder. You can still buy them here, a bushel sack for fourteen dollars. I did. Do you have any idea how much hard work is needed to grind a whole bushel of peppers?

Next you come to Radium Springs. This is a very small town, which includes a Family Dollar store, and that is about it. No grocery store, no laundromat, not even a gas station. Still, it is only fifteen miles to Las Cruces, by back road or Interstate, which has everything. But Radium Springs is home to the

Leasburg Dam State Park, which is one of the better ones. In addition to the hot showers, it also has free wifi. It is set in fairly flat desert, amidst profuse desert life, most especially an abundance of rabbits, and a wide variety of birds. The Fort Selden Ruins are located here, and the Leasburg Dam, the first diversion dam built on the Rio Grande.

All through the Winter, the river was impounded in various reservoirs, preserving the precious water for when it would be needed. This is when the Rio Grande, the Big River, is reduced to a mere trickle. In many places, you can step over it and not even get your feet wet. Then comes Spring, when the saved water is required for irrigation, for thirsty pecans and peppers. Then the gates open, and the Rio Grande lives up to its name.

Now we have run out of towns. There are a few farms and ranches, and several clusters of houses, but from here on, the land becomes more and more wild. A couple of pecan groves, a few pepper farms, and several crossings over the river, then you enter the untamed country.

Untamed for now. The grovers are making some new inroads upon it. The national economy is improving, as evinced by the dozens of new groves. There are a few that are a couple of years old, more that were just planted this year, and even bare fields, freshly levelled, with stakes driven in rectangular arrays, ready to receive the new saplings. It takes years for a pecan tree to grow large enough to produce a profitable harvest. The grovers are clearly confident enough in the future to make

their investment now, and a lot of it.

Along the way, you come to a Border Patrol check station. It strikes me as a mighty poor place for such a thing. There are three routes north through this area: This one, I-25 paralleling it a mile to the East, and another to the West that comes out at Hatch, ten miles to the North. 185 and I-25 pass through Las Cruces; anyone smuggling could easily offload there. The other route is more direct; but there is another station there.

Beyond the station, the land is virtually untouched, virgin desert, a few scattered creosote to show the natural state, clouds to tease the land with rare rain, and sometimes a rainbow, just because.

Here the land is truly wild. Sometimes, at long intervals, there will be a house or a shed. Not farm houses, for there are no fields. No, there is no apparant reason, no need for any building. Perhaps they are country homes, residences for folks who work in Las Cruces. It would be pleasant to have a place of such beauty to truly escape from the city, at least for a few hours each day. Someday, perhaps, the chile fields and pecan groves may encroach upon this area, but their absence now is not a question of economy or demand, but of water. There is only a certain amount available, and it is all being used already. The ongoing climate change is likely to bring more rainfall; if so, the croplands will expand, but not otherwise.

The highway ends at Hatch, which is also my main reason for taking this road. Hatch is a must-visit place, at least if you are a connosieur of chile peppers. New Mexico is the Chile Pepper Capital of the World, and Hatch is the Chile Pepper Capital of New Mexico. Just ask the residents; they will tell you so. They hold a Chile Pepper Festival every Labor Day weekend, which I cannot properly describe for you, primarily because I have never attended it. But in early October you can buy dried red chiles and freshly roasted green chiles from the recent harvest for very good prices. This is where I bought my bushel of red chiles for fourteen dollars. (It is not that I cannot buy them elsewhere, the same peppers from the same harvest. There is a significance, almost a religious attitude: This is Hatch; I get my peppers from the source, the wellspring.) I remove the stems and strip out the seeds and ribs, and grind the body for my chile powder. I grind the seeds and ribs separately for supercharger. Most of the heat is in the seeds and ribs, so I use the body for flavor, then adjust the heat with the others. I can do a mild chili or hot from the same peppers.

While you are there, visit the Village Market. While it is mainly a supermarket, they have several pieces of vintage farm equipment, restored to shiny almost-new condition. Quite a contrast to the usual rustbuckets in local museums and fields.

And so ends New Mexico Route 185. A short run but, as I said, including all of the conditions from urban to untouched Wilds. The only road I know of that is at all similar is the route from Los Angeles to the Angeles forest, and that one comprises several roads and much more abrupt transitions. This one is smoother, quieter, and cleaner. It just does not get any better.

US 82

It does not look like all that much, not on the map. Only one hundred and six miles between Artesia and Alamogordo, with half a dozen villages along the way, Hope, Mayhill, Elk, Wimsatt. It trends quite straight East to West, but aside from the first quarter inch (on the map; maybe twelve miles on the ground) it is nearly as twisty as the Mississippi River. And there are premonitory signs along the way, ominous "Abandon all hope, ye who enter here" warnings. It all starts off with a rather weather-beaten alert: "Highway 82 is under construction. Be prepared for delays." This is followed by a rather scary sketch: A short flat line at the top labelled "Cloudcroft 8,650", a steep drop to another short horizontal, "High Rolls 6,000", then another drop to "Alamogordo 4,000". Very ominous, when you consider that I am reading this sign at an altitude of thirty-four hundred feet. Over the next ninety miles, I am going to climb almost a full mile upward, and you can just bet it is not going to be a slow and steady rise. No, I am expecting a long level with a few ups and downs as the plains roll, maybe a thousand feet rise to the foothills, then a hard low-gear pull to the pass. As I roll along, this impression intensifies, because I see this sign repeated at least three times, maybe more. I can not be sure, because on the road, my attention is so absorbed in the wonders of the landscape that my remaining intellect is only capable of "one, two, three, many, lots". But the point is, this kind of warning is typical, to prepare truckers for what lies ahead. But repeating it, especially repeating it at least four times . . . Well, I have never seen that before. Maybe one repetition of "6% Grade", but no more than that. The road ahead must be very hairy, even dreadful. I know that I am somewhat anxious about tackling it, what with towing a trailer behind me, but I am also rather eager. I know the bike can handle it, though I may have to downshift a couple of gears. But I like twisty mountain roads. Especially when there is little traffic, such as I am seeing (or rather, *not* seeing) now.

For it is not a heavily travelled road. Every five or ten minutes a vehicle will pass going the other way, but so far, no one has overtaken me. I am running just under the speed limit, but almost everyone else speeds, five or ten miles per hour over the limit. I see no semis at all, and just a couple of big-rig RVs. One motorcycle, and she was stopped in a pullout. I started to pull over, but she signalled she was okay, so I kept moving. The villages were little things, none with as many as a hundred inhabitants. Still, each one cut the speed limit down to thirty-five, though one was only for a couple of hundred yards. Many farms and ranches, but far more cows than two-legs.

The road itself was fine, a clean two-lane asphalt, with no potholes and very few tar-filled cracks. It was not a new surface, not newly-laid black, but the usual weathered and faded gray. A little roadkill, all small critters, and half a dozen thrown retreads off on the shoulder. No wrecks, none of the usual crosses commemorating fatalities. Curvy, but not twisty. I mean, the curves were big. Cruising along to the West, the road does a uniform quarter-circle to the South, taking a full mile to do it, then another smooth quarter-circle back to the West, using another full mile. It really is an easy road, and a good one for sight-seeing, because so little attention is required for the actual driving, and so much needed for the views.

There were very few spectacles, just an overall peaceful, bucolic beauty. Lots of new-mown hay aroma, and after the first ten miles, no more crude oil. That is the real downside of Artesia; it is a nice town, but it is apparantly the central clearing house for the southeast New Mexican oilfields, and always smells (stinks) strongly of petroleum. Why, even in Brantley Lake, twenty five miles south, the oil smell is pretty strong when the wind is in the North. But today the wind was in the South, maybe a little East. No stenches. The flora helped on that score, too. It has been quite a rainy Summer, for New Mexico. I had noted it on the way South last week, and it was even more remarkable today. I am sure you can visualize the grassy plains in late Summer and early Fall: Magnificent amber waves of grass stretching off as far as the eye can see, rippling and waving in the wind, ripe and ready to fall, to make room for the next generation. That is the way it is, usually, but not this year. It is not amber. It is green. Some parts are sort of half-and-half, but this stretch is green, all green, some areas lush and lustrous green. The cattle love it! Also the deer and the pronghorns, who are numerous.

And it is about this time that I notice I am up over five thousand feet, and only a third of the way. At this rate, there will barely be a thousand feet to fight near the pass. So what is it with all of these warning signs? The road goes on, the landscape continues with little variety. It is quite boring to tell or be told about it, but elegant to experience. The weather is right, little wind, and that mostly behind me, though it is starting to get hot. I am looking forward to the coolth of the pass. There are few clouds, much in contrast to the day before. I am actually running a day behind schedule, which schedule called for me making this passage the day before. But on Wednesday the weather was rainy, with thunderstorms in the mountains through which I am about to pass. I have ridden through such weather when I had to. I will brave anything but a blizzard when I must. (Or maybe a tornado.) But I do *not* have to. Nobody was expecting me. (Well, actually, they were, but I called ahead and told them I was taking it easy. They said they had figured I would.) So here I am in clear, quiet weather, in wondrously pastoral peace, rolling the world behind me as I slowly, imperceptibly climb towards the sky.

It was not till about ten miles short of the pass that the climb finally became obvious. The speed limit dropped, the curves became tighter, the upgrades steeper. The road was now clearly a mountain road; no more broad vistas to either side, no more far-distant horizon. Now I was among hills and cliffs and cuts into the mountainside. I even had to downshift to fourth gear a couple of times. And the air was noticeably cooler, even growing cold, especially when the capricious mountain winds shifted to blow straight into my face. Riding the mountains requires more attention on the road and the bike, more control, more actions to maintain one's course. It is very different from the peaceful relaxation of the plains, but better in that it is more varied and wild. It is a pity that this has to happen just when the landscape becomes more interesting, but that is how it is, and it is of no use to moan and complain about it. It is much better to find the good aspects and enjoy them, even rejoice in them. Dwelling on the downside is completely uprofitable and unpleasant. Why do so many people seem to revel in it?

Finally I reached the pass. Cloudcroft and its suburb or companion or wannabe, Cloudland. There is a ski area up here, probably a resort of some sort. Poor folks, they had no snow last year. None. But this year should be better, maybe the best in living memory. The signs are quite favorable. Certainly it is cold. Or it feels cold. The temperature is probably in the low fifties, but since I just rose from the high eighties, it feels colder. Regardless, it is a welcome change.

And there it is: The Pass. It is all downhill from here.
Very downhill. Speed limit thirty-five. Runaway truck ramps
every few miles. Steep. This is what the admonishing signs
foreboded. This is the plummet. I fell from the Cloudcroft
peak two thousand feet to the High Rolls ledge, bounced off
and toppled two thousand more into Alamogordo. Well, okay,
not *quite* that precipitously. But I switched off the motor and
coasted for the next fourteen miles, almost all of the way to
Alamogordo. There were a couple of slight rises, but sheer
momentum kept me up almost to the speed limit. There was a
lot of braking, but by switching between front and rear brakes,
I avoided any danger of overheating. The speed limit of thirty-
five was relaxed to forty-five, then fifty, though for trucks, it
stayed at thirty-five. I even saw a truck on one of the runaway
ramps. Then the limit went up to fifty-five, and I had to restart
the motor. The city spread before me. Only eighty miles or so
left to my trip.

All in all, it was a very pleasant road. I am looking
forward to riding it again, but next time, east to west. *That* will
be interesting. The long but short climb, four thousand five
hundred feet in fourteen miles, will be a strain. I expect I will
have to do most of it in third gear, maybe even second for the
worst parts. Many drivers will be upset with me, many curses
will rain down (or up) upon me, as the following vehicles are
constrained by my snail-pace climb at thirty or even twenty-
five miles per hour. Fortunately there are many passing lanes
on the upward-bound side. But once I am at the top, there will
be the long and leisurely ride, out of the mountains, through the
foothills, and rolling along the rolling prairies. I really do have
to try that next Spring. It is such a beautiful road.

But, you know, even though it was a Wednesday, I never
saw a single construction worker all day.

Santa Fe Trail

Almost two hundred years ago, there was an international trade route that ran between Franklin, Missouri and Santa Fe in New Mexico. It was known, naturally enough, as the Santa Fe Trail. It was only a mule trail, and later a wagon track, carved out by hundreds of sets of hoofs and wagon wheels.

There had been several attempts to establish trade between the East and Santa Fe, but political conditions brought them to nothing; Spain still owned the country, and insisted (as colonial powers will) that any trade must profit the mother country. Starting about 1725, several French expeditions reached Santa Fe; some lost their trade goods along the way, and were not molested, but those that did succeed were arrested and their cargos confiscated. Not many tried after that, until Spain bought the Louisiana Territory from France in 1762, and a Mexican, Peter Vial, tried opening routes from St. Louis, Missouri, San Antonio, Texas, and Natchitoches, Louisiana. Again, political interference prevented success. Several parties from the young United States, notably one led by Zebulon Pike in 1806, were arrested in Santa Fe by the Spanish authorities and, again, had all of their goods confiscated.

But in 1821, the Mexicans rebelled and succeeded in kicking the Spaniards out. They *wanted* trade, so it was a whole new ball game. There was a depression in Missouri at the time. A young man (31 years), a saltmaker, named William Becknell was in debt, and feared he would soon be arrested, for this was long before modern times, and being in debt was not considered normal and even honorable. He knew well that every prior attempt to trade with Santa Fe had proved ruinous, but his desperation was such that he somehow put together a mule-train of goods, and set out from Franklin, Missouri, with five companions. He hoped to make a hefty profit, and he succeeded right well. It took two and a half months, but on November 16, 1821, he reached Santa Fe and was welcomed by the governor, who encouraged him to do it again. Many Americans emulated Becknell (the Missouri depression was still going on), and quite a few Mexicans started running the route the other way. At least, they brought silver to Missouri and bought goods to carry back to Mexico. The trade was so lucrative that it ended the depression in Missouri, even though the depression had spread to the rest of the United States. And thus was the Santa Fe Trail finally established. It flourished for almost sixty years.

Trade was so brisk that it only took a couple of years to saturate the Santa Fe market. This did not daunt the traders; they simply did not stop in Santa Fe, but went on to other Mexican cities, even as far as Mexico City itself. This is mighty ironic, since it was half again as far from Mexico City to Santa Fe as it was from Missouri to Santa Fe, which is a large part of the reason the Santa Fe Trail was needed in the first place. Some of the Mexicans working the route did not stop to purchase their goods in St. Louis, but went on to Philadelphia, New York, or Boston, or even as far as London and Paris! You could say, justifiably, that the full Santa Fe Trail extended from Mexico City to Paris, nearly seven thousand miles.

Becknells route went through the Raton Mountains, including Raton Pass. This later became known as the Mountain Route. It was not too bad for the mules who carried the freight. He returned by a more southerly course which was later called the Cimmaron Route. It was also a little bit shorter, 890 miles versus 934 for the Mountain Route. Forty four miles may not seem much, but it was several days' travel, and almost as important as avoiding the mountain trails. Many parties soon followed his southern trail. There were a few places where someone took an alternate route he thought might be better, but the vast majority used the original tracks. Beside the tracks through the grass, the route also came to be marked by broken and sometimes burned wagons, by the skeletons of horses and mules and oxen, and the graves of people who died along the way. It was not an easy journey. Water was usually scarce, and the Indians who inhabited the lands through which the trail passed were often hostile, either because they resented trespassers, or feared that the strangers might drive them or the game away, or from desire for the goods in the heavily laden wagons. Or even just for the fun of fighting these new folks. The army was kept fairly busy protecting the route till the Mexican-American War broke out. Then the US Army was off fighting Mexico instead of the Indians, so the Cimmaron Route became too dangerous, and traders went back to the Mountain Route. As I said, it was acceptable for mules. Wagons were another story altogether. Steep mountainsides in Raton Pass forced the wagons into the valley and canyon bottoms, where they had to fight their way through the mountain streams, and any improvements made were washed away the next Spring. But an enterprising mountain man, one Uncle Dick Wootton, built a road through at his own expense, including many bridges and cuts, and the route became far easier. Of course, he charged tolls of all travellers, and that is a story in itself!

After the war with Mexico, the Army went back to work negotiating with the Indians, and traffic went back to the old Cimarron Route. Until the Civil War. Again the Army took off to do something "more important", the Indians took advantage of their absence, and the Santa Fe traders took the Mountain Route. And Wootton made more money.

The trail was heavily used for many years, not only as a trade route, but later as a migration path, a way to get to California. But then the railroad came. In 1863, the Union Pacific Eastern Division Railroad started building west from Kansas City. Year by year the western terminus extended, taking the start of the wagon route with it. On February 9, 1880, the first train entered Santa Fe, and the old Santa Fe Trail, November 16, 1821 to February 9, 1880, age 58 years, 2 months, 24 days, was no more. The iron tracks, which followed the old trail in some places, almost completely superceded the old wagon road, and it slowly faded away. The wheel ruts were flattened and filled in by the hooves of wild animals, and smoothed out by the rain. The skeletons of draft animals and the remnants of broken wagons decayed and crumbled, slowly sinking into the ground. The crosses and grave mounds melted away, and today there are very few traces surviving. Only a few very rare wheel ruts remain.

Modern highways now carry the local traffic and the long distance carriage not travelling by train. In many places, the new highways follow the old trail, often lying exactly along its path. I am riding one now, a stretch of some sixty miles. It is marvelous, and I do marvel that I traverse in ten minutes as much distance as the old wagon trains would cover in an entire day, and a good day, at that. It is wonderful, and I do wonder at the conditions that obtained, and the difficulties the old time muleskinners had to overcome. For example, the plain is pretty much flat, and what slopes there are are long and gentle. The first users, the makers of the trail, avoided anything steep, and selected the gentlest gradients available, so all that the later travellers had to do was follow the tracks. But the plain is not *entirely* flat; there are gullies and washes scattered about, and since the trail is skirting the Sangre de Cristo Mountains, all of the run-off from the mountains flows perpendicularly across the trail. The gullies can be deep, ten, fifteen, twenty feet, and their banks are almost always steep, much greater than forty-five degrees. They had to be crossed, they *were* crossed, but the crossings, any signs of them, are long gone. Some washes are wide, ten or fifteen times as wide as they are deep. I can see, in imagination, the wagonmen hard at work with picks and shovels, breaking down the bank, digging a cutting into the plain and using the dirt to pile up a ramp within the gully. On the near side, they build it as steeply as their animals can safely lead the wagons down; on the far side, the ramp must be much more gradual, and thus much longer, but laid out as steeply as the beasts can drag their loads up it. The way back was usually easier, as the wagons and oxen were often sold in Mexico, but if they were kept, the teamsters might have to rework the steep side, making it shallower, but there is a pretty good chance they will have to do the whole job over again, if there was a flood that caved in their cuttings and washed out their ramps. Rivers and creeks were probably less of a problem. They might have to do more work to make the cuttings to get down to the river, but there would be no ramps to get washed away, so there was little chance of having to repeat the work. Just touch up the cutting a bit, if that. On the other hand, the rivers out here are often muddy, so one has to wade into them to find out what the bottom is like, and how deep it is.

Rivers also presented another problem: Sometimes they flooded. Heavy rains in the mountains could make the river a raging barrier that simply could not be crossed. The whole wagon train would have to sit there and wait for the water to go down. No doubt the draft animals enjoyed it. They would get a few days off to graze and rest. Probably not too big a deal for the men, either; they were in no particular hurry, and certainly were in no danger of running out of water! A few days added to the months that the whole trip required was not important. For the emigrants heading west, though, it could be critical. They usually had a deadline for getting through the mountains before the snow made them impassible. You have probably heard of the Donner party, attempting a new route too late in the year, getting caught in a blizzard, and losing many of their people. (It is a little-known fact that Jim Bridger, the famous Mountain Man, had a commercial interest in this new trail, and advised the Donners to take it. Half of the party stuck to the old trail, and made it through with no problems.) So the plains travelers were advised to always cross rivers *before* making camp. If you had already crossed, then you would not be delayed if the river happened to rise during the night.

The way was long and hard. They had to get up early, eat, and harness their teams. Then drive all day, often walking beside the wagons when the going was rough, perhaps pushing them or turning the wheels by grabbing the spokes and heaving when the ground was wet and muddy, building ramps in the gullies, all in the hot, shadeless sun. There was also the hazard of broken wheels and axles. Spares were carried, but it took time to do the repair, and that, of course, delayed everyone. It was not safe to leave a lone wagon behind to catch up later. They could only travel some ten miles, on good days, because the animals could not pull the heavy wagons very quickly, and they had to stop to make camp several hours before sunset, because they needed time to unharness and let the animals graze and water. It took a lot of grazing to feed the animals, for the wagon trains did not carry fodder, needing all of the space for trade goods, and those big beasts required a *lot* of food. Sometimes, on rough ground, and when the going was all uphill, they might only make a mile or two in a day.

And now, here I am, casually cruising a smooth and well-maintained hard-surface highway, with permanent bridges over every gully and wash and river, covering in a single hour more distance than even the fastest wagon train could manage in a week. In the distance I see a freight train rolling along, perhaps only half as fast as my bike, but hauling in its long train of cars more weight of cargo than was carried over the Santa Fe Trail in an entire year, and only needing a half dozen men to drive it. This is progress, *real* progress. So much less effort required, so many man-hours freed up to do more important things, such as travel just for the sheer fun of it. Manual labor replaced by machine labor, so people can think and create art and new things. I have known many people who regret the modern world, who condemn "progress" as a bad thing, who long for the "simpler" life of the "good old days". Progress is not a bad thing. Technology and machinery are not evil or disruptive. They cannot be, for they cannot think or feel. Only the uses to which they are put can be bad, and that is the fault of people, certain individuals who are greedy or foolish or, usually, both. The simpler life of the good old days required harder labor for less return, in a world that was much more hazardous, a world where infant and child mortality was appalling, where life was often brutish and short, a barbaric world of ignorance and disease. Life is much better today, at least in most nations, and improving for more and more people every day. Sure, there are problems and injustices; there always have been, and maybe always will be. But overall, things are much better. The tale of the Santa Fe Trail is only one example.

It is a good day to live.

Raton Pass

The Vikings had a *kenning*, or saying:
> *Evil is known as soon as it comes.*
> *Good, when it goes away.*

Very wise, and just as pertinent today as it was a thousand years ago.

Traveling between Raton, New Mexico, and Trinidad, Colorado, you traverse Raton Pass. It is fairly steep. Big rigs slowly fight their way up, and cautiously grind along in lower gears all the way down. But aside from that, the passage is quite easy. The road is, after all, an Interstate Highway. There is even an RV camp and cafe with showers, a playground and laundry facilities, at the top of the pass. This is good. This is also not noticed particularly. But if it went away . . .

A hundred and fifty years ago, Raton Pass was an alternate route of the Santa Fe Trail. It was actually on the original route, the one William Becknell used on his historic first trip to Santa Fe. It was favored because it was safer than the regular trail, with a much lesser risk of Indian attacks, but it was dreaded for being longer and more difficult. The fact that most travelers usually used the main route in spite of the danger should give you some idea of the difficulty of the pass. I am going to give you a better idea.

At first, it was traversed by mule trains. Mules can go anywhere, and generally do. But even for them, the trail was not easy. These are, after all, mountains, and there was quite a bit of climbing and descending, and the grades were often steep, and the slopes along which they ran even steeper. The trail had to wind around boulders and through streambeds, and was usually not very smooth at all. Later, most freight was hauled by wagons, since a wagon drawn by four mules (or oxen) can carry many times the weight that the animals could carry. It was a lot cheaper, most of the way, but not necessarily when crossing the Pass.

Many wagons did not make it. Shattered rigs and broken pieces lined the trail, and the skeletons of hapless draft animals. Not a few graves, as well. The road was steep, and very rough. Rockslides altered the way pretty much every winter, and the first parties through in Spring usually had a substantial amount of digging and rock rolling to do. Actually, I am sure every party did, but the ones in Spring had more, largely because much of the wagon road was in the bottoms, where the spring floods rearranged everything every year, washing out any trace of the road, rolling even the largest boulders into the way, and piling up logs and driftwood at every curve. Accounts by the pioneers describe the strenuous trek to the pass, the bitter cold in Winter, the sweltering heat in Summer, with the teamsters pushing the wagons as much as the beasts were hauling them, often doubling up teams, or more, to get half of the wagons up, then repeating the trek with the other half. Many days they only progressed half a mile, or even less. And once they had reached the top, they had to face the perilous passage down. Those who are unfamiliar with mountain travel do not realize that traveling uphill is easier than going down, on foot, on horseback, or in a vehicle. The road is just as steep, but you cannot simply coast on down, because if you go too fast, you cannot stop. If a wagon gets away, it will continue on till it smashes against a cliff or rolls over the edge. It will often roll straight over the animals hauling it, or, if they are harnessed behind, it will drag them right off their feet. There are accounts of wagons with all four wheels locked so they cannot turn at all and a dozen men holding the wagon back, slowly skidding it downhill. And making a half mile progress that day.

An old mountain man, known as Uncle Dick Wootton, saw an opportunity here. He obtained charters from Colorado and New Mexico to build a road over the pass, and proceeded to do so. He blasted out ridges and hillsides, built long grades and dozens of bridges, felled giant trees, and eventually finished a good road, easily traversed by wagons and stagecoaches. Then he charged a toll. It is interesting to note that he never had any problems with the Army or the American freighters; they were accustomed to the idea of toll-roads. Nor with the Indians, though for a different reason. The Mexicans, though... As Uncle Dick put it:

"With the stage company, the military authorities, and the American freighters I had no trouble. With the Indians, when a band came through now and then, I didn't care to have any controversy about so small a matter as a few dollars toll! Whenever they came along, the toll-gate went up, and any other little thing I could do to hurry them on was done promptly and cheerfully. While the Indians didn't understand anything about the system of collecting tolls, they seemed to recognize the fact that I had a right to control the road, and they would generally ride up to the gate and ask permission to go through. Once in a while the chief of a band would think compensation for the privilege of going through in order, and would make me a present of a buckskin or something of that sort.

"My Mexican patrons were the hardest to get along with. Paying for the privilege of travelling over any road was something they were totally unused to, and they did not take to it kindly. They were pleased with my road and liked to travel over it, until they came to the toll-gate. This they seemed to look upon as an obstruction that no man had a right to place in the way of a free-born native of the mountain region. They appeared to regard the toll-gate as a new scheme for holding up travellers for the purpose of robbery, and many of them evidently thought me a kind of freebooter, who ought to be suppressed by law.

"Holding these views, when I asked them for a certain amount of money, before raising the toll-gate, they naturally differed with me very frequently about the propriety of complying with the request.

"In other words, there would be at such times probably an honest difference of opinion between the man who kept the toll-gate and the man who wanted to get through it. Anyhow, there was a difference, and such differences had to be adjusted. Sometimes I did it through diplomacy, and sometimes I did it with a club. It was always settled one way, however, and that was in accordance with the toll schedule, so that I could never have been charged with unjust discrimination of rates."

Uncle Dick charged a dollar-fifty per wagon and a nickel per beast. This was before 1870, when a dollar was a good day's pay, comparable to about eighty dollars today. Would you pay an eighty dollar toll to drive over a ten-mile pass? Not today. But it was well worth it back then, because it cut several days off the journey between Trinidad, Colorado, and Raton, New Mexico. Wootton, of course, got quite rich from his road. There is even a town near the pass named for him. Are you getting an idea of just how evil this pass was? Half a mile a day (admittedly, not *every* day), hard labor for maybe a week or more, and a pretty fair chance of not surviving it. Well worth paying a day's wages to use an easier, though still difficult and dangerous, road.

Another testimonial to the expense people were willing to put up with to cross Raton Pass was a vehicle purpose-built just for traversing the trail. It had treads for overcoming the roughest terrain, and a powerful motor to drive them (steam, of course; or so I assume). It even carried a cannon, forward mounted, probably to blast and break up especially large boulders in its way, though it would have served quite well should any hostile Indians attack. Very rare, but it was known to happen. This vehicle was very advanced for the time, and undoubtedly expensive, but it was perfectly adapted to the dire canyon, and could pull several regular wagons behind it. It is on display in a park in Raton. I am not completely certain that it was built to conquer the pass, but as there is no descriptive plaque attached, I have had to conjecture. There is no doubt that it would have done the job.

One of the most beautiful sights there is, especially to the hardy (weary) pioneers of the mid-nineteenth century, and most especially before Uncle Dick built his toll road, is the southern end of Raton Pass. You have been working your way for days through hills and valleys, not on our smooth modern road that is cut into the hillsides to provide a more uniform grade, but, usually, down in the valley and canyon bottoms. The hillsides lay at thirty or forty degrees, often much more; a mule would have no problem, but you could not drive a wagon across them, not even straight up or down. No, you had to get right down into the relatively flat bottoms, where the rolling boulders and landslide debris lie. You must roll them aside, or build a path around them suitable for your wagons. All by hand, mind you.

Gradually, you fought your way to the Pass, then slowly worked your way down, always with cliffs and peaks looming on all sides. The view each day was the same as the day before, and it was hard to believe you were making much progress at all. And then, one bright day, you round a ridge, and the view expands before you. You see hills on either side, the valley meandering among them, but off there, still miles away, is the plain. The land is *flat*. It is smooth. It is perfectly level, and you can see the Trail running straight across it. True, it is not *really* flat, not free of gullies and rocks, but it *looks* like it, and compared to the Hell you are now in, it is a city street. In another two or three days, with luck, you will be there, and the Raton Pass ordeal will be over. Just the idea itself is enough to get you drunk.

Remember this when you drive over the pass, safely and comfortably seated in your air-conditioned car, exerting yourself only to turn the steering wheel, to press lightly on the accelerator or brake pedal, and only taking ten minutes to pass through. For free. This is what we call "good".

Scene:
Chimney Rock

We have far too many National Monuments. A monument is something to commemorate a person, thing, or event; it says so in the dictionary. It should not be diluted into a device for political machinations. The San Gabriel Mountains National Monument used to be the Angeles National Forest. Then the President changed it, probably to please the eco-simps.

In Colorado, at a bit less than eight thousand feet, stands Chimney Rock. It is really not all that spectacular; I have seen many more beautiful rock formations. But it is distinctive, a truly unmistakable landmark, and thus was of great value to pioneer movers. Now it is, rightly, a National Monument. It commemorates the men, women and children (do not forget the children!) who fought their way to a better life with stubborn persistence and courageous determination, and thus built a nation. (The weak and timid turned back, or died on the way.)

It is not much to look at, but what it stands for is epic.

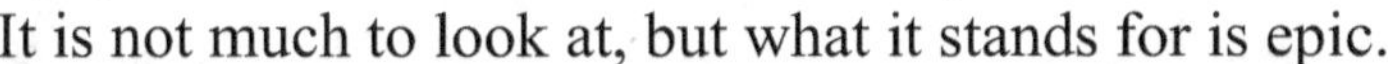

Scene:
The Great Divide

The Great Divide is a line of high ridges running north to south across the continent. It is generally not the highest points in the area, but all along the way, rain falling on one side flows to the Pacific Ocean, and on the other, toward the Atlantic. Or at least, to the East. Mostly. Except that sometimes the Divide splits for a ways, and you have an intermediate area, a basin, out of which the water never flows. Okay, it is a couple of thousand miles long, and this is just one small part of it, but this piece is spectacularly representative of the entire length.

It lies in the Rocky Mountain National Park, and is easily the best part of the Park; this scene alone is enough to justify a visit. Standing over eleven thousand feet, just above the timber line, it is surrounded by higher peaks, and looks down across great glacial valleys, filled with evergreens and elk. The road itself is closed in winter, not so much by policy as by snow.

Scene:
Ames Monument

The Ames Monument commemorates Oakes and Oliver Ames, who were instrumental in building the Union Pacific Railroad. It lies a mile or so south of I-80, using the same exit as for Vedauwoo. It seems like a poor location for a monument, not being near anything, but when it was built, it was close to the railroad, and is close to the highest elevation on the UP (8247'). Nearby was the Dale Creek Trestle, the longest (706 feet) and tallest (125 feet) bridge on the UP; but the bridge would sway dramatically in the Wyoming winds (and, believe me, those winds can be very fierce!), and if the train went more than four miles per hour, empty boxcars were sometimes blown right off. Eventually the rail route was moved a few miles, to avoid the worst snowfalls, and the monument was left behind, along with the town of Sherman, a quarter mile from the Monument.

The monument was constructed of granite blocks, some weighing as much as twenty tons, which were quarried about a half mile away. It does seem, at first glance, to be a rather odd shape, but when you compare it to the natural formations in the area, it fits right in. Designed by Henry Hobson Richardson, a prominent architect of the time, it is said to be one of his best works, and I must agree. It certainly is beautiful, but it is also almost unknown. I have yet to meet anyone who has even heard of it, much less seen it.

I-90

Interstate highways tend to be something less than scenic. *Tend* to be. One of the exceptions is I-90 between Sundance, Wyoming, and Rapid City, South Dakota Why? Because this is the part that passes through the Black Hills. If you are familiar with the Black Hills, that says it all.

Okay, if you do not know them, maybe you need a bit more. The route is spectacular, but quietly so. There are no steep grades, no sharp twists or turns, no towering canyon walls nor infinite plains, nothing that shouts aloud and grabs your attention. Even Bear's Tepee is beyond the horizon. No, this land will not introduce itself to you. It is not shy, but it is serene. You have to make the first move. You have to notice it. And it is not at all difficult to ride the whole eighty miles and not see a durn thing.

It is difficult to describe properly, because there is nothing *particular*, nothing that stands out. It is the whole thing, the entire view, the complete landscape, the cumulative effect. A cent is trivial, but a hundred thousand million of them in one pile is a billion dollars. This terrain is the esthetic equivalent.

Granted, the road is much marred by billboards; it is, after all, a major tourist destination. Rapid City has a presidential theme, Sturgis is all about motorcycles, Deadwood stresses outlaws and "Wild West", Sundance celebrates its one outlaw. But if you can get past the distractions, if you can see beyond the obvious, past the hundred-yard right-of-way, you will find the real world.   Wildlife is abundant, deer, elk, turkeys, woodchucks. Woodlands and meadows, pastures and hayfields

abound.   Bedrock outcrops protrude from the fields, sudden gullies pierce the bright red soil, surrounded by vivid green grasses and thickly wooded hills. Those hills themselves stand in all shapes, rounded, flat-topped, conical, smooth and craggy. But there is something else, something not exactly of this world, a peace, a serenity, as if the land knows itself, knows its purpose, and is utterly satisfied and content, and has no desires or needs beyond what it has, and what it is. It is perfectly willing to share with you, and cares not a whit if you choose to not notice. All of the Indian tribes in the area recognized this, and held the Hills to be a sacred place. I-90 touches the surface, but no more. It gives you a chance to be introduced to the possibilities. You can follow up, look farther and deeper. Or you can yield to the commercial distractions and get the T-shirt, or just drive straight on through. Your choice.

I-90 is only a teaser, a trailer, an advertisement. Choose to leave the highway. Choose to take the back roads into the Hills themselves. Sure, see Mount Rushmore, especially from inside the tunnel (you will know it when you see it). See Crazy Horse. Visit Hill City, especially the fabric shop with its nineteenth century fans. But also go deeper, go beyond the settlements and historical sights. Go into the woods, visit the more remote campgrounds. There, if you are patient, if you know how to look, how to see what is actually there, you just might begin to understand why the land is sacred. If you get up with the sun at Custer Trails, if there is no wind, and the mists are rising, there is a pretty fair chance the land will talk to you. Listen carefully, for it is very wise.

Scene:
Vore Buffalo Jump

Modern myth says the Indians used every part of the bison. The truth is, they had a use for every part, and sometimes, especially towards the end when bison neared extinction, they *did* use every part, out of sheer desperation. But before that, when the beasts were abundant, and before they had horses with which to pursue them, the Indians were often extremely wasteful. One of their favored tactics was to entice or trick a small herd, sometimes hundreds of animals, into running over a cliff. Then they could harvest robes and meat and whatever else they happened to need at the time, but only what they could get before the rest rotted. It was not a large percentage.

Vore Buffalo Jump is one such place. It is a large sinkhole in the middle of a plain, right by I-90. In fact, it was discovered during construction of the Interstate. Starting around 1500 CE (probably when the sinkhole formed), many tribes in the area began using the Jump as a trap. They kept using it for three hundred years. They used existing gullies as fences, and supplemented them with long rows of rocks. They would come back year after year, probably different tribes at different times, to fill their larders in preparation for Winter.

Only about ten percent of the Jump has been excavated so far, but the information learned is significant. There is a small museum there, and frequent guided tours of the actual excavation; the digging is funded by tour fees. It is quite fascinating, educational, and fun. And after the tour, they teach you to use the atlatl, a spear-thrower that preceeded the bow. It is not at all difficult; even the kids can soon kill a target.

Bozeman Trail

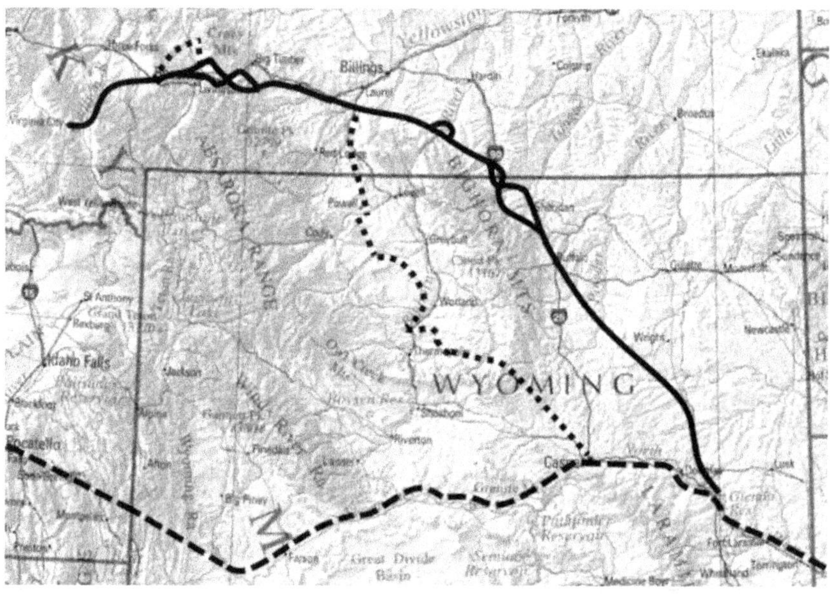

In 1862, large gold deposits were discovered on Grasshopper Creek in Southwest Montana. Word soon reached the East, greatly exaggerated as such reports always are, and a gold rush started. In 1863, John Bozeman and John Jacobs scouted a route from Bridger's Ferry on the already well-established Oregon Trail to Virginia City, Montana, which was named the Bozeman Trail. In 1864, the route was largely modified and improved by Allen Hurlbut. But the name was not changed. Many wagon trains followed the trail to the goldfields. Many Indians resented this, and proceeded to harrass the emigrants.

The result was quite a lot of treaty-breaking, but in this case, it was largely the Indians doing the breaking. In the Fort Laramie Treaty of 1851, the tribes in the area agreed to stop fighting each other, and to allow the United States to build roads and forts through their area, and the United States agreed to keep White folks out. Well, the tribes did not stop fighting, or not for long, and the Army did not keep settlers and miners out, and as a result of the settlers' inroads upon the game, especially the bison, the Indians started attacking them. By the time gold and silver were discovered in Montana, the treaty was pretty well shredded, and the Indians had no qualms about raiding the wagon trains. The really odd thing is that the Bozeman Trail went through the lands of the Crow, and the Crow were the only tribe to *not* dispute the trail. In fact, they sided with the Whites. Of course, this may be because the Arapahoe, Cheyenne and Lakota had invaded the western Powder River , and by 1860, had driven out the Crow. Maybe they figured that by helping the White Man, they could get the land back, or at least weaken their enemies enough so that *they* could take it back. An Army Colonel asked Jim Bridger to scout out an alternate route to avoid hostile Indians. He did, but it was not a very good route, with large stretches lacking water and grass for the livestock. The Bridger Trail never got more than a quarter of the traffic of the Bozeman Trail.

The Lakota maintained that they had driven out the Crow, and thus, by long tradition, they now owned the land. Therefor the Whites had to dicker with the Lakota for permission to use it. The Army disagreed, and the result was Red Cloud's War. One event in the war was the Fetterman Fight, in which, on December 21, 1866, Captain William Fetterman and a force of eighty men were lured into an ambush. Two thousand Lakota wiped them out to the last man, taking about twenty minutes.

Sort of a dress rehearsal for Custer and the Little Big Horn. You do not hear much about this war. The Indians won, and the Bozeman Trail was shut down. Fewer than four thousand settlers had crossed the trail.

The Bozeman Trail was very well scouted, so well that much of it is still in use today. In Wyoming, I-25, from Douglas to Casper and on to Buffalo, runs south and west of the Bozeman, but Wyoming Route 59 follows it fairly closely from near Douglas to Bill. Then it took a fairly straight route to Buffalo, a route that is not used today. I-90 from Buffalo via Sheridan, Wyoming to Wyola, Montana is very close to the original Trail route. It is then abandoned till about Columbus, where I-90 picks up on it again, and follows it to Bozeman. Montana 84 and 287 then follow it to Virginia City.

People usually envision these pioneer trails as an endless pair of wheel ruts stretching from horizon to horizon. They were not like that at all. The ruts could be hazardous and difficult to negotiate, so wagons tended to spread out; the trail, the actual land which the wagons rolled over, could be a mile wide. Only in a few places such as river fords did all or most of the traffic follow the exact same path. A few of these places are still visible, with clear ruts (some as much as five feet deep), along with trash and debris left by the early settlers. (Litter is no new thing; it has a long history.) They are not on main roads, some are on private land, but if you really want to see them, they are there. If you just want to see old ruts, and do not care which trail they belong to, visit Independence Rock. It is easily accessible, and well worth seeing just for itself, and includes clear Oregon Trail ruts.

Scene:
Big Muddy

Cruising Interstate 25 near Glenrock, Wyoming, you will pass south of what once was the Big Muddy Oilfield. From its initial twenty-six barrels per day production, it grew to be the tenth-ranked oil field in Wyoming. Today, gazing out over the non-descript valley, you can count the one remaining ancient walking-beam pump (not operating the day I was there), but on the far away surrounding ridges to the North and West, there are hundreds of windmills industriously spinning, extracting a different sort of energy from the same land. The wind in Wyoming will never run out.

Middle Popo Agie Falls

There is a trail you will not want to miss, running six miles from a parking area near Bruce's Bridge to the Falls of the Middle Popo Agie. It is rated as Very Difficult, though I would call it only Difficult. Wear your boots, and bring along a staff, water, and anti-bear gear. And a camera. I have never seen a bear up there, but one year there was fresh bear scat on the trail when I returned. It had not been there on the way up.

The trail follows the north side of the Middle Popo Agie River, heading west towards the wilderness area. The canyon carved out by the river is fairly broad, with the river fifteen or twenty feet wide, until both narrow abruptly at Bruce's Bridge. At its lowest, the river flows well over one hundred cubic feet per second. Picture a cube of water five feet on each side, passing you every second. During the Spring Runoff, it can be five times that, or more. Rocks recently fallen from the cliffs are rough and sharp-edged; boulders in the stream are mostly smooth

and well-rounded. Far to either side of the stream are boulders and smaller stones as weathered as those in the river; in the Spring, they *are* in the river, for then it is broad, and powerful.

The pitch of the river is steep, and will grow steeper as you follow it west. It is filled with rocks, and small falls are frequent, though most of them are only a foot or two high. There will almost always be at least one in view, but these are *not* the Falls of the Popo Agie. Those lie farther upstream, and are bigger. Lots bigger. But take a good look at the water. If you want to touch it, do it now, for there will be no further chances. This is the closest you will get to it for the rest of the hike. Unless you leave the trail and climb down. Down a near-vertical rock cliff. It can be done, but bring a stout rope and a friend.

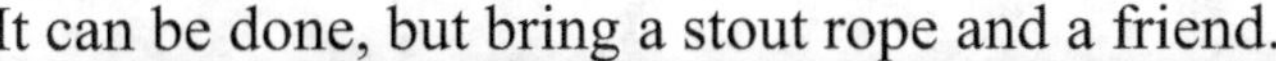

The river will often be in sight from the trail, but not close. Not far away horizontally, but from this point on up, it runs in a canyon within the canyon.   Vertically, it will be far below. Mostly, it will not be visible. This is the time for looking at the rocks and the cliffs.

At some places it is difficult to decide if one is in a canyon or a valley. Not here. Here there is no ambiguity at all; this is clearly a canyon, with vertical walls and raw, unweathered, sharp-edged rocks. Also with many that are not at all recently fallen, but, being above the highest waters, are only worn by ice and lichen. Some of the cliffs make me wish I was a rock-climber; there are chimneys and sheer faces that look like such grand fun to ascend!

The trail is often rough. It is not level, and it does not steadily rise. Rather, it rolls, up a ways, then down somewhat less, up again and down, up and down. The surface is rarely smooth; opportunities to twist an ankle are profuse. At a few places you will want a stout staff to aid your balance, for you may need a few seconds to place a foot firmly on rocks that will not roll. Take it slowly and pause frequently, for much of the time you will need your full attention on your footing, with nothing to spare for sightseeing. Fortunately there are several good rocks for seating. You will want to stop to take pictures, which is a good excuse to rest without admitting you are resting. Must keep up appearances, you know. Also, you should look backwards frequently, for the view back is, as usual, quite different from the view forward. Granted, you will

be coming back this way, so you will see the other trail then, but why not see it twice? It is well worth it. The river is far more visible looking back than it is looking forward, and you can see both cliffs and water at the same time. But have a care approaching the edge; some of the rocks may be unstable, and it is a long and rough way down.

Eventually you lose sight of the river completely. The land is dry and arid. It would be easy to believe there is no river for many miles.

The trial is narrow, and dusty, guarded by standing stones as it wends its way through clumps of sere bunchgrass. Far above, you notice for the first time a great sphinx guarding the trail up, and realize she has been watching you all of the way.

After a while, you will come to a shoulder. The trail winds behind it, away from the river, but before you follow it, take a good look. You can see the river below, and also a few glimpses above. This is what you came for. This is your first view of the Falls. But this is only a glimpse, a mere hint of things to come. The phrase is overused, but this time it is true: You ain't seen nothing yet. Turn your back on the river. Walk around the rock.

The soil is thin and weak, and slabs of bedrock break through like the dry skull of a poorly preserved mummy. The trail is paved, sort of, with almost randomly placed irregular rocks. It must be for erosion control, for they certainly do not improve footing. Quite the contrary! But where is the water? Where are the falls?

And suddenly we see them. We top a rise, and there is a wide overview, two falls encircling an island of bedrock. A wide moraine fall lies to the left, and a narrower one on the right. The land is suddenly green and lush, and even before we descend to the water, the air feels cooler and damper. Perhaps it is, but again, it does not compare with what is yet to come.

Many of the famous waterfalls are simple, though no less beautiful for their simplicity; the water flows over a cliff and drops straight to the bottom, like Shell Falls in Wyoming's Bighorn Mountains. Some are a bit variegated; Niagara Falls has Horseshoe Falls and American Falls. Wedding Veil Falls in Utah boasts two drops and a moraine. Monkey Falls in Arizona has two twin channels. But this fall, the Middle Popo Agie Falls, has them all: Moraines, straight drops, sheets, multiple streams, Class 20 rapids.

The observation area is wide and deep. There are several paths through it, and a picnic area. At no point does it descend to the river itself; during the Spring Thaw, the river is quite deep, and all of the "improved" area is well above the high water mark. It gets close enough, and there are comfortable benches where you can relax and immerse yourself in the view.

There are a few oddities as well. Perhaps the strangest is the uppermost fall. It is a simple wide drop from what looks like a flat and level slab of bedrock. A sheet of water curls over the edge and drops straight to a pool. But if you look at the trees in the background and the foreground, you may note that they have a different vertical. According to them, the water is *not* falling straight down. Very peculiar!

There is also a great troll lurking in the river. There is a footbridge nearby; perhaps he is watching it, hoping for a big gruff billy goat to come along. Trolls are known to be very vindictive, and they have long memories.

The footbridge is not to be missed. It is at the extreme end of the trail, beyond the benches. There were some very foolish hikers on the benches the last time I was up there. It appears they had underestimated the trail and overextended themselves. They were getting well-rested before tackling the trail back, and absolutely refused to go a single yard farther, much less the hundred yards over the bridge. What a pity!

It is a very simple bridge, stout and narrow. You could not roll a wheelchair across it, but that does not matter, for you could not get a wheelchair up here short of packing it on your back. Sorry, folks, but this sight is not handicapped-accessible. But the bridge does give you another view angle on the falls. Between the first view around the corner of rock and the view from beyond the bridge, you get at least one hundred twenty degrees difference. From there, you can see straight up the western branch of the river from the patient bathing troll to the not-vertical waterfall.

This is also the coolest and most moist area of the Falls. Here you find the little, non-spectacular, falls. I have seen many bifurcated falls: The stream leaps out, strikes an outcrop, and two streams descend from there. Here we have the opposite: Two small streams fall and meld into one. Beside it is a scene worthy of a fine Japanese garden. A wall of bedrock, split into blocks that yet remain in place, sports miniature shrubs clinging to cracks, and miniscule blankets of spongy moss. Tiny trickles seep from crevices and tinkle into a quiet pool.

It is a long walk to get there, and just as long to get back. You are already tired from the uphill hike, but, of course, it is all downhill from here. Well, mostly downhill. As I said, the trail does roll a bit. But you are a seasoned hiker, and you are accustomed to it. Enjoy the view, It is actually prettier on the way down. Perhaps you can look back, and this time recognize the sphinx you did not notice before. Be respectful to her. As far as I know, she has never eaten anyone, not yet, but why should you take the chance?

Scene: Crowheart Butte

The Fort Laramie Treaty of 1851 defined the tribal lands in central Wyoming, and required that the tribes stop fighting each other. The Indians soon violated the treaty, and the Arapahoe, Cheyenne and Lakota took the Powder River area away from the Crow. Later on, in 1866, the Shoshone and Bannock fought a battle here with the Crow for control of the hunting grounds around the Wind River Basin. Once again, the Crow lost.

On the north side of US 287, near the village of Crowheart in the Wind River Reservation, stands Crow Heart Butte, named for the battle in which the Crow were driven out (though most of the fighting was miles north of the butte). It is so named because the victorious Shoshone chief Washakie bore the heart of a Crow on his lance in the celebratory War Dance.

Washakie was one of the greatest figures in American history. He was a great leader and a mighty warrior, and a far-sighted statesman. Through his actions and wisdom, he saved his people's lands from encroachers both Red and White.

South Pass

When I was a young lad, fourth or fifth grade, I was entranced by the stories of the Noble Heroes of American History: George Washington, George Custer, Jim Bridger, Thomas Edison. Being young and naive, I believed the legends. I later found out that the tales were mostly allegorical (that is, they were fiction written to make a point, by what we, today, would call "spin-doctors"). Two-dimensional portraits that were at best vastly incomplete, and often outright lies. Washington did not exactly lie, but he did twist facts for his purposes; he was a politician. Custer was mostly victorious against helpless victims. . . I mean, enemies. He is mostly known for his biggest (and last) blunder, disobeying orders and attacking early, planning to take all of the credit for a great and "glorious" victory which would carry him to the Presidency, seeking a weak enemy who turned out to be superior in every respect. Bridger loved the wild lands, but he was out for profit above all else. He persuaded half of the infamous Donner Party to use his new California trail (for which he had a monopoly on selling supplies). Edison was a brilliant organizer, whose hundreds of employees did the actual development of inventions for which he took the credit. And the profits. Perhaps these men were noble, but only in that they were like typical European nobility of the last millenium.

I do not mean to imply that these men were villains (except possibly Custer), or that they did not contribute heavily to Society (again, except possibly Custer). They, and many others like them, were clever, even brilliant, men who perceived and took advantage of opportunities, and to a large degree built the United States. Angels, though, they were not. But then, who is?

Among the tales of Jim Bridger, notably in the book "Fur Trappers of the Old West", South Pass plays an important role. It was much sought after, and hard to find, because it was described as "a pass that does not look like a pass". It was said to look like "a long, treeless valley". Maybe it did. Maybe it didn't. The thing about these children's books is, they are mostly propaganda, not intended to enlighten children, but to lead them into thinking the way society's leaders *want* them to think; the alleged facts in them must be verified independently, not blindly accepted as Gospel Truth. For example, I was confused as to why this was called South Pass, when it lay two-thirds of the way up the continental United States. But it did lie in the southern part of the primary fur-trapping lands, when one remembered to include Canada. Okay, so South Pass is an appropriate name, when looked at in full proper perspective.

In all of my travels in the Rocky Mountains, I had always passed east or west of South Pass; my wanderings had never led through it. This is not odd, considering how big the Rockies are, and what a bounty of wondrous and beautiful sights permeate the entire area. But today, at long last, my path would lie through South Pass. I could see it with my own eyes, and compare it with the doubtful legends, and finally know the truth. Riding Wyoming Route 28, I climbed the eastern slopes, the same basic route that Jim Bridger had used, higher and higher, closer and closer, eager to dispel the political history, twisted and spun to abet some twisty and spinning selfish agenda. The path lay through a long valley, but far from treeless. And they were not young trees, either. Clearly, this forest, and many of these very trees, had been here two hundred years ago, appearing very much as they appear today. Jim Bridger himself had looked upon some of these trees. I passed Atlantic City (population thirty-seven). I passed South Pass City (population thirty). I reached South Pass, a gap between two modest peaks. It did look sort of like a pass, but only a minor one. I topped it and looked, like the bear, for the other side of the mountain. But it was not there.

The land beyond was flat, at least, by mountain standards. Far, far off, dim and blurred with haze, distant peaks saw-toothed the horizon. If I had ventured into this place uninformed, I would have looked to that horizon for the Pass. North and south, more peaks bordered the land. And between lay a plain. It could be called a valley, since it lay between mountains, but by my standards, it was too broad. It was a plain, a typical rolling Wyoming plain. At seven and a half thousand feet. And there were no trees. Almost none. It was long. It looked like a plain. Or a valley. But it was not. It was, indeed, a pass, and it definitely did not look like a pass.

I rode on, across the low plain. An altitude of nearly a mile and a half may not seem low to you, but remember, this is the Continental Divide. One could argue that the South Pass is actually many miles wide, There are towering mountains to the East and the West that rise almost twice as high. There are long ridges and plateaus a thousand feet higher. But this is the line that parts the waters. This is the line that forces the waters back to the Pacific Ocean. They will pass around the higher peaks and ridges, sometimes flowing east for a while, but always trending west, wending their way to the sea. Actually more south than west, through ponds and reservoirs and canyons, including Grand, till they debouch into the Gulf of California, and then, finally, to the Ocean. It would be a truly great adventure to ride with the water all of the way. But I do not seek adventures. Adventures kill people.

This plain that is a pass is open range. There are a few cattle picking their way among the spherical olive-colored bushes to browse on the tall brown grass. Rare raptors circle constantly, seeking the rodents that creep and cower below. The air is fresh and clean, its scent spicy, reminiscent of cedar, and with a musty overtone like old books. The Sun is warm, and the only wind is my wind of passage. Dark clouds abound, but the rain reserves itself for the distant mountains. The Road lies straight, and runs on forever. Time stops, for only details change, and few of them. My vision from the Tales was much narrower, two, perhaps three miles wide, a valley gouged between peaks, and clearly descending. Reality is a plain, as much as twenty miles wide, and as well as I can tell by eye, not descending at all. This is what Jim Bridger saw, two centuries past. It is still here. It has not changed. He did not pause at the summit, gaze forth and say "Oh, looky! This must be South Pass!" That is what the book said happened. Not those exact words, but the realization while standing in the mouth of the pass that he had Found It. No, he saw only a dry plain, a sort of plateau, no habitat for beaver or other fur. He rode on to the mountains in the West, still intent on finding the pass that lay behind him, and it was probably not until the next day that he realized he was going downhill, and that the streams did not trend eastward. Only then did he look back and realize he had found South Pass, and passed right through and beyond it. If I had lacked a map, I would have done exactly the same.

I understood, now, the truth behind the legend. It made me feel as if I was a part of History. You will likely feel the same.

The Great Divide

Everyone knows about the Great Divide, sometimes called the Continental Divide. At least, I have never met anyone who had not heard of it. It runs from the North to the South through Alaska, Canada, the continental United States and Mexico, right down the spine of the Rocky Mountain complex, then carries on through Central America and along the Andes in South America all of the way to the tip of Tierra del Fuego. Rain on the west side flows to the Pacific Ocean, and on the east side, to the Atlantic. As with pretty much everything that "everybody knows", this data is only about half right. For one thing, while it does part waters into East and West, none of the eastward flow is into the Atlantic.

The Continental Divide only runs to the end of Mexico; the part in the Andes is the South American Continental Divide. It is, after all, on a different continent. The whole thing, from Alaska to Tierra del Fuego, is the Great Divide. We cannot call it *the* divide, and should not call it the *Continental* divide, because there are a half dozen others, mostly running more east and west than north and south. In the North is the Arctic Divide, running northeast and passing west of Hudson Bay, directing runoff into the Arctic Ocean. A few hundred miles south of that is the Laurentian Divide, starting in Glacier National Park and running east, and passing just north of the Great Lakes. Waters north of it flow into Hudson Bay and Baffin Bay. Branching south from it is the St. Lawrence Divide, passing south of the Great Lakes and the St. Lawrence River, and branching off of that is the Eastern Divide, which runs south along the Appalachian Mountains and the center of

Florida. Waters that fall east of the St. Lawrence and Eastern Divides flow into the Atlantic, but waters west and south of the Eastern, St Lawrence and Laurentian Divides (that is, waters that flow east from the Great Divide) drain to the Gulf of Mexico. So, you see, waters that run down the east side of the Great Divide do not flow to the Atlantic, but to the Arctic Ocean and the Gulf of Mexico. Not until you reach South America does any runoff from the Great Divide go to the Atlantic (the Central American runoff is into the Caribbean Sea). Floccinaucinihilipilificators (it is a real word, honest; it means those who state that a thing is worthless. You know, nitpickers) may argue that the Gulf of Mexico flows into the Atlantic, but by the same argument, so do the waters of the Pacific Ocean, through the Arctic and Antarctic Oceans. It may take a few thousand years, but they do eventually get there.

There are also a few anomalies, basins where the waters go to neither ocean, ever. Streams, even rivers, flow into them, but nothing flows out. The Great Basin, which is, very roughly, the State of Nevada, lies within a divide of its own, a more or less oval shape. Precipitation occuring outside flows to the Pacific, but what happens in the Basin, stays in the Basin. And, of course, we have the Great Salt Lake and the much smaller Salton Sea, which have inflows but no outflow. Both were once much larger than they are now, but their inflows are much reduced. The Rocky Mountains at one time were a great deal wetter than they are today.

This Great Basin itself never touches the Great Divide, but there are several others, three major ones, that do. The biggest one, about one third the size of the Great Basin, lies in Mexico between the Sierra Madra Occidental and the Sierra Madre Oriental (in English, the West Mother Mountains and the East Mother Mountains). The mid-size one comprises about half of the New Mexico panhandle and a bit of Arizona, with the bulk in Sonora and Chihuahua, in the Sierra Madre Occidental.

The smallest of the three lies in Wyoming, just south of South Pass, about one hundred miles long and fifty miles wide, something under five thousand square miles. I-80 touches on the south side, and US 287 cuts through the eastern end. Other than that, there are three tiny settlements on the edges and half a dozen dirt roads crossing it. Nothing else. If you can handle rough dirt roads, and you like truly wild beauty, it is well worth visiting. It is a wilderness area. It has not been designated an official Wilderness Area, and is not protected as such areas are, but apparantly it is not necessary. Very few people visit it, or even know it exists. But it sure is wilderness!

You cannot travel the length of the Great Divide unless you are a skilled mountain climber. As you ought to expect, it crosses many mountain peaks, right across the summits. Some are over fourteen thousand feet! You can hike within a few miles of it, with permissions for wilderness areas and such. It cuts right through Rocky Mountain, Yellowstone and Glacier National Parks. For the most part, you could follow it exactly. It is, after all, the ridgelines, and they are usually the easiest paths. The obstructing broken rock and dense brush lie on the hillsides and especially in the valley bottoms. Only the occasional cliff or deep ravine would force a detour. The views would almost always be spectacular.

Do not try it in Winter, though!

There are no roads that follow the Divide for more than a couple of miles, if that, but many cross it. Usually there will be a roadside sign giving the elevation, and often a parking area, to indicate where the road crosses the Divide. Many of them do not appear any different from a hundred other passes and, actually, *are* no different; they just happen to lie on the Divide.

   The best one I have seen is in Rocky Mountain National Park, one of the most beautiful and magnificent Nature sights you can find. On one side spreads a vista of range after range of bare rock and snow-capped peaks. If Lewis and Clark's Corps of Discovery had followed that route, they surely would have despaired at the sight. "You want us to go *there?* You expect us to walk through *that?* I'm going home!" But to the other side is a gorgeous glacial valley, half filled with forest, half with tundra, for this pass lies a bare hundred feet above the

timberline. The valley holds a small lake, fed from the snow still melting from the ridge on which you stand. If you are lucky, as usually happens here, you may see a herd of elk by the lake. But it is much farther off than it first appears; the elk appear so tiny, they are at first very hard to spot. You really need binoculars to watch them. They do serve very well to show you the scale of this sight. Everything appears smaller than it is. That little puddle really is a lake. Many of the trees are over a hundred feet tall. On a very clear day, you can see mountains over a hundred miles away. Maybe this pass is a bit higher above the trees than I thought.

The unimaginative will say it is only a ridge, and not truly important. So it happens to divide the waters. What is such a big deal about that? Well, you just go see it. *Look* at it, really *look*. It is not just a ridge, it is the Great Divide, and it is a *very* big deal.

Scene:
Castle Wall

I love rock formations, cliffs and boulders, arches and balancing rocks, carved into eldritch shapes by wind or water or ice. Few, though, are unique. This one is, and also very little known.

Eight miles east of Alpine, Wyoming, on the north side of US 89, just east of Wolf Creek Campground, stands the formation I call Castle Wall. Ages ago, the stone strata, laid down flat as all strata are, was twisted intact through ninety degrees. Erosion has washed away the softer stone on either side, and left two vertical walls about ten feet apart. They look just like the wall of a castle, two walls of dressed stone, filled between with rubble and cement. It once ran up the entire hillside. Now only a few yards remain. I have seen nothing like it, anywhere.

Utah Route 150

There are many routes to enter Utah. From the South and Southeast, you can ride through the wind- and water-carved rocks, the landscapes that most people envision when they think of the Beehive State. From the Southwest you can immediately enter the vast forests, or from the West, enter the wide deserts. From the North you can arrive almost immediately in the tamed metropolitan area that surrounds Salt Lake City, or the brilliantly red canyons of Flaming Gorge. But between these last two lies my favorite: Route 150.

It starts in Evanston, Wyoming, bearing the same number, though here it is Wyoming 150. Some twenty miles, over high plains gradually becoming forest, takes you through Wyoming highlands to enter the Wasatch National Forest and Utah. This is high montane forest, the trees thick but short. You rise and rise, twenty five or thirty miles on a winding road, more on a hilly high plain than the expected cliffs and valleys, till you reach the pass, over eleven thousand feet, near Mount Agassiz. At twelve and a half thousand feet, it is not the highest peak in the state, that being Kings Peak forty miles east and eleven hundred feet up. But it will do.

It has been a fine ride to this point, through very pleasant country, with several excellent outlooks. There was also a ranger station, always a good thing to visit. If you plan to camp around here (and you should), do stop in and ask for any news or updates, such as fire conditions, any restrictions and such. Also thank the staff for taking care of your forest. It is yours, you know. But good as the road has been, the pass is where the real fun begins. The twenty or so miles down to Kamas are a solid expanse of easy, peaceful arboreal paradise, especially in August and September. A large percentage of the trees are aspen, mostly in large groves rather than spread uniformly. When aspen leaves change, they become bright and brilliant yellow, orange and red, quite unlike the faded pastels of most other trees. The autumn leaves of New England are a beautiful sight, but they lack the vibrancy and mass of these aspen. For one thing, you never know what colors the leaves will assume. The weather conditions and the state of the trees' health have a lot to do with determining the colors. A given tree may be yellow one season, then red the next, and a year later, orange. Or a single tree may flourish all three colors at once. You simply cannot predict it.

Great swaths of color drape the hillsides, intermixed with the various shades of evergreens. If you time your passage well, you will see on your descent the entire gamut of aspen display, bare branches at the summit, then undropped brown, evolving into random patches of yellow, orange and red, and at the bottom, leaves still green. One year I caught it so perfectly, that the next day I rode from my camp up to the summit and back, just to experience the leaves again. Alas, the data chip in my camera went bad, so I lost all of the photos. But that just gives me an excuse to go back, some day. I am very skilled at finding excuses to do what I want to do.

There are several fine campgrounds along the road, from Stillwater north of the pass to Beaver Creek near Kamas. Between them, at the low end, is Shingle Creek, which, unlike Beaver Creek, has a beaver colony, a very large one. It boasts

many fine beaver dams and several ponds. In fact, it is almost a textbook overview of beaver construction: Retention dams to make ponds, diversion dams to redirect flow, and wing dams to enlarge ponds. All assembled, very skillfully, from the local aspens, which the beaver also eat. If you camp in this area, do stay at Shingle Creek, and devote a full day to exploring this complex; it is several miles long. There are also deer, elk, and the ubiquitous coyotes and chipmunks.

The town of Kamas, at the terminus of Route 150, has a gas station with a mini-mart, but no grocery store. For that, you need to go another fifteen miles to Heber City. It is also a good base camp should you need to go to a city. Salt Lake City is about forty miles from Kamas, and of course has everything. Including a sky-glow that ruins stargazing at Shingle Creek.

This is also a good jumping-off place for the Fishlake and Manti-La Sal National Forests, as well as all five National Parks in Utah, and Great Basin National Park in Nevada. You can get to any of these in one day.

All told, Route 150 is one of my all-time favorite roads.

Scene:
Bridal Veil Falls, Utah

You have probably seen Bridal Veil Falls, but I do not know in which state. There are several falls by that name. All that I have seen are very tall and narrow, and usually present a lacy white face.

This one is on the south side of Utah Route 92 between Orem and Charleston. It falls from a high hanging valley in three stages; first are two free plummets, then the namesake foamy flow down a steep talus slope. There is an Indian Romeo-and-Juliet legend associated with it, which is where it got the "Bridal Veil" name. I think it rather inappropriate, as I am not aware of any Indian tribe that used bridal veils. The legend aside, from appearance alone, I would have named it Horsetail Falls.

But who cares, really? The Falls are magnificently beautiful under any name, especially during the spring thaw. They must have been flowing for a very long time, because they have carved a huge, wide notch in the cliff. It is impressive when seen from the highway, but do drive down to the base. The view from there is stupendous.

Scene:
San Rafael Reef

On I-70, which is also US 50, just west of Green River, Utah, you will come to San Rafael Reef. You cannot miss it, as the highway has been driven right through it. There is a large observation area just to the West. The Reef, also called the Eastern Reef, is a part of the San Rafael Swell, 2000 square miles of awesomely rugged beauty. You could spend several delightful weeks just wandering the many trails and canyons.

Pretty much everything you can find in the justly famous Utah National Parks also exists in the Swell, plus a few extras.

For example, there is the Cleveland-Lloyd Dinosaur Quarry, which includes the world's biggest deposit of Jurassic fossils. Then you have the Ghost Rocks at Ghost Rock Summit, which is also right near the Interstate. There are many canyons to hike: Eagle, Devils, Spotted Wolf, Little Wild Horse, and Little Grand. Some trails are easy, some difficult. Several dirt roads cross the area, and most of them are passable for a street car. With four-wheel-drive, many more are available.

The whole area is accessible year round, but can be *very* hot in the summer. Bring lots and lots of water, because there are very few amenities in the area. It is mostly BLM land, where camping is free, but there is no water, no toilets, no trash collection. There is also no cell phone service, so you will need to do your research ahead of time, and get printed maps. Also a desert survival kit. And water. Did I mention water? Well, I will again. What you bring is all you will have.

Well south of I-70, and requiring several back roads to reach, is Utah's Goblin Valley State Park. It has twenty five campsites, at $30 per night plus a $15 park entrance fee. This includes free water, showers, toilets, dump station and trash collection. Also two yurts, each $100 per night, but providing heat and air conditioning and an outdoor gas grill with free propane. You might do dry camping most of the time, with a night at the park every few days to replenish your water supply and grab a hot shower. Or buy water at one of the more or less nearby towns. Remember, no water available outside the park and the towns.

But do be wary of flash floods.

Arizona 67

It is not much of a road, just about forty miles worth, running south from Jacob Lake campground. Which incidentally is even less of a campground than 67 is of a road. Much better is DeMotte, about twenty-five miles south. It lies in the Kaibab National Forest on the Kaibab Plateau, about one hundred eighty miles by road from Grand Canyon Village. There are a lot of trees, but mostly they lie pretty far from the road, well separated from it by a spare grassy meadow. A few intriguing rock formations accent the fields, and there are many aspens, so it can be colorful in the fall. But it only goes to one place, and the only way out is back the way you came. So why should you bother with it?

This is why. It is called the North Rim of the Grand Canyon.

Beats the South Rim all hollow. Sure, the South Rim has gift shops and book stores and an IMAX theater. It is by far more accessible, and well worth seeing, but there are really only a few views. It does offer access to hike (or ride) down to the bottom. Or ride a helicopter over it. It is big, but lacks variety. Seen one view, you have pretty much seen them all.

The North Rim has more to see, like about ten miles of accessible rim. You can see all the way down to the Colorado River. See it down there? It is barely discernable from the South Rim. It seems deeper, perhaps because it drops off faster, perhaps because you can see trees far below, and you know they are not mere bushes. It seems wider, probably because there is less clutter in the way. There are many more enchanting rock formations, not so far off that you can only see the outlines, but right up close.

There are stepped Mayan temples, smooth Egyptian Pyramids.

There are long wandering walls, and sharp jutting turrets.

There are buttressed cathedrals, and crennelated castles.

There are ancient ruined walls; one even has a window.

You can look down to strange sculptures, or even farther into dizzying depths that seem to call to you and pull you down.

Truly, there is no comparison. The South Rim is grand, no doubt about it, but the North Rim goes beyond grand, far, far beyond. It is only a pity that it is so much more difficult to reach. But that only enhances the appreciation, for a thing easily obtained is little valued.

I have only touched upon the wonders of the North Rim, and I have not even done that much for the Visitor Center, or described the restaurant. One of the paths to the Rim is a living, natural botanical garden, filled with local flora and descriptive signs. I have not mentioned the official names of formations, such as Angel's Window. And I am not going to.

You will enjoy it more if you imagine your own names. This essay is not a substitute for a visit. The idea is to encourage you to make the trip yourself. I have shown you so little, and that little in weak, tiny, flat pictures. I cannot show you the size; there is not a paper big enough. I cannot show you the depths, only let you know that they are there. Sure, visit South Rim. It is only nine or ten miles south-southwest. But from there, you will have to drive one hundred eighty miles to get here. Take US 89 and 89A. See Marble Canyon and the Vermillion Cliffs and the vast red plateau to the south. They alone make the trip worthwhile. And when you finally reach Arizona 67, perhaps you will be lucky. Sometimes the Grand Canyon extends itself into the sky.

Scene:
Marble Canyon

Many, many people have seen Grand Canyon, but most have only seen it from the South Rim. Far fewer have been to the North Rim, which is, in my opinion, much better. Two problems, though: North Rim is often inaccessible in Winter, and even when you can get there, it is a hundred fifty miles out of your way. From anywhere.

Fortunately, there is a consolation prize: US Alternate 89, running east from Jacob Lake, is most impressive. The last twenty miles skirts the aptly named Vermillion Cliffs. They are, and so is the sand eroded from them, which makes up the entirety of this desolate and savagely gullied plain. And at the end, when the Road crosses the Colorado River, is Marble Canyon. It is odd; this is the same Colorado River that carved Grand Canyon, meandering twenty miles left and right, and cutting over a mile down, a cross-section twenty five thousand times that of this fairly straight bed only a couple of hundred feet wide and deep. Is the rock here that much harder? Or did a greater force carve out Grand Canyon? I do not know. But it sure is pretty.

Envoi

Writing these essays is one of the most pleasurable activities I have. Publishing them is another story. They have to be sorted, then laid out and assembled to meet the standards and conventions of modern publishing, and a table of contents written (and I am most truly thankful I do not have to build an index). The cover must be created, designed and laid out to exacting specifications. Then the whole thing must be read, carefully, looking for typos and other errors. That part is fun. Once. But then it must be done again, and again, and even then one cannot be sure that everything was found. But eventually the book is complete, and my baby is all grown up and leaves the nest and becomes available for sale. It is finished. Ended.

But there are two consolations. First of all, the tales are now being shared. Others can read them, be entertained, and, hopefully, learn something of value, something that will help to improve their lives, even if only in a small way. Second, I can embark upon the next volume. There are always tales left over, articles that did not quite fit in the latest book. And, of course, there will be several more that were inspired and written while the publishing was in progress. More of them will come over the course of the coming year, and next Autumn there will be another book to do, or two, or three.

The Road is my home, and it is there that I can learn new things, most of them quite obvious, at least once they have been noticed. I will visit new places, some which I never imagined could exist. I will wonder at new sights, be joyed at finding old friends, and always gain new insights. And from these things come new essays. They are all out there in the sunrise, patiently waiting for me, and the Road is calling.

I am going home.

About the Author

The Lonesome Hillbilly is a wanderer from birth. Born in the Lone Star Republic (but not in Texas), he traveled a thousand miles by his first birthday, and ten thousand by his second. He lives on a motorcycle, and in a tent he made. He has been in every state of the Union, plus Asia and Europe. Politically he is a Rational Anarchist. Spiritually, he respects all religions, and no churches. He winters in the low deserts of Arizona, and tours all New Mexico during the Spring. The rest of the time, you will find him somewhere within five hundred miles of the Rocky Mountains. Probably.

Stay Free!